Growing up Catholic

IN THE GEOGRAPHICAL CENTER OF NORTH AMERICA

In memory

of

My grandmother

Magdalena Senger Bertsch

CONTENTS

IN THE GEOGRAPHICAL CENTER OF NORTH AMERICA

FAMILY TREE

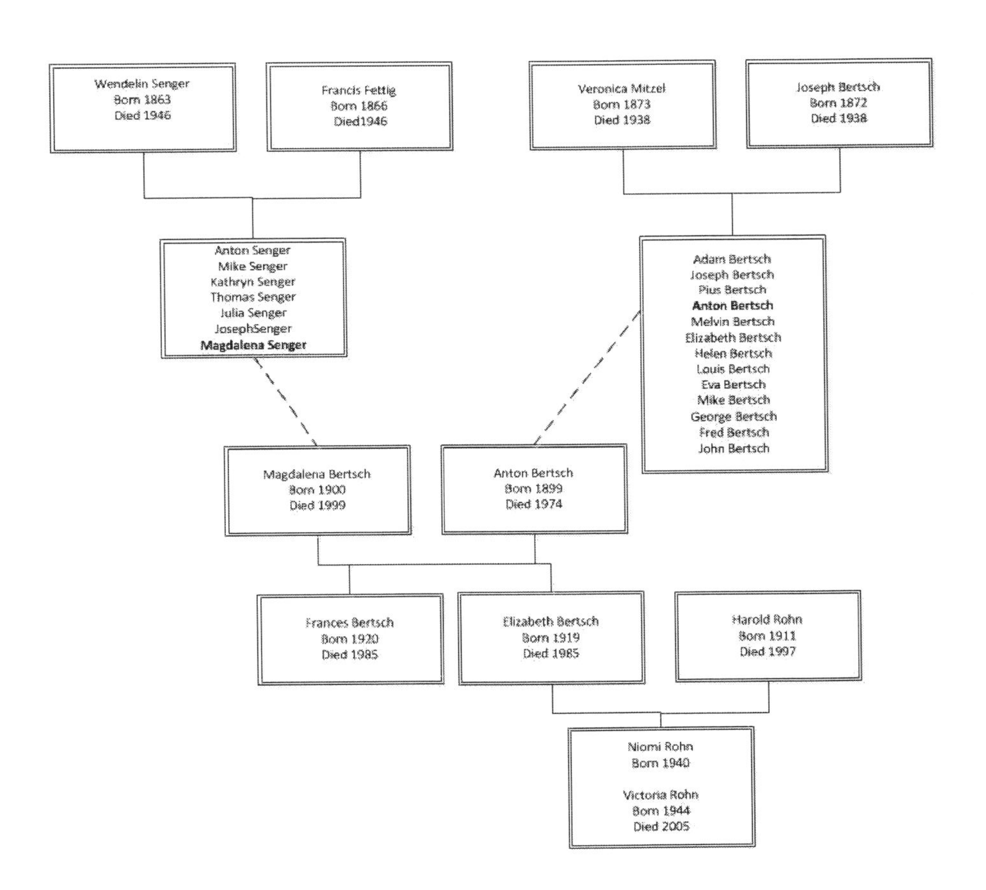

Wendelin Senger
Born 1863
Died 1946
Francis Fettig
Born 1866
Died1946
Veronica Mitzel
Born 1873
Died 1938
Joseph Bertsch
Born 1872
Died 1938
Anton Senger
Mike Senger
Kathryn Senger
Thomas Senger
Julia Senger
JosephSenger
Magdalena Senger
Adam Bertsch
Joseph Bertsch
Pius Bertsch
Anton Bertsch
Melvin Bertsch
Elizabeth Bertsch
Helen Bertsch
Louis Bertsch
Eva Bertsch
Mike Bertsch
George Bertsch
Fred Bertsch
John Bertsch
Magdalena Bertsch
Born 1900
Died 1999
Anton Bertsch
Born 1899
Died 1974
Frances Bertsch
Born 1920
Died 1985
Elizabeth Bertsch
Born 1919
Died 1985
Harold Rohn
Born 1911
Died 1997
Niomi Rohn
Born 1940
Victoria Rohn
Born 1944
Died 2005

Growing up Catholic

IN THE GEOGRAPHICAL CENTER
OF NORTH AMERICA

HOME

In my town, where the wind whipped needles of dirt in your face
on hot summer days and needles of snow in winter,
life was Work for farm kids before school and after school
when they were allowed to go to school,
and the German-Russian farmers
talked about their cows and their women in the same breath,
judged each other by the size of their barns
and the number of boys (a baby every nine months and ten minutes
Mama said)
dropped by *the old lady,* the name for *wife* no matter her age,
who tied a babushka around the metal curlers in her hair,
took her cream and eggs to Schaan's grocery,
then waited in the car parked in front of Andy's Tavern where
her man *who wore the pants in the family*
was drinking beer and vodka
after confession on Saturday night.

We were sixteen miles south of
the Geographical Center of North America
Main, Volga, Lublin, and Kiev Streets;
First, Second, Third, and Fourth Avenues,
a square town with clear boundaries
—religion, gender, nationality—
Our Lady of Mount Carmel Church on the north end of Main,
on the south end, the Soo Line depot and the railroad tracks—
the way out.

Published by *Dust & Fire,* 2008

1

GERMANS FROM RUSSIA—
ME AND MOM AND GRANDMA

Mom was obsessed with leaving Balta after what Dad referred to as her "run in with the Nuns." Her confrontation with Sister Mary Dominic, the school principal, and the community censure that followed put fire in her blood. She scoured the "Help Wanted" advertisements in the *Grand Forks Herald* for months and found Dad a job.

In August 1953, the summer after my 8th grade, and after nine years in Balta, Mom and Dad put the last boxes in the trunk of the old Hudson. A few days prior to this final moving day, they had borrowed a flat-bed truck from a farmer friend and moved the furnishings of our apartment behind the Farmers Union Oil Company store in Balta to an apartment above Ella's Beauty Shop on Main Street in Park River, North Dakota. My eight-year-old sister Vickie and I tucked our fragile, china, story-book dolls around us in the back seat, and we left Balta.

Dad's quiet hope for the future—a nine-to-five work day with every other Saturday off, and maybe enough money "to make ends meet," infected me as much as Mom's exuberance. I all but bounced up and down on the car seat on the way out of town. Forget catechism, the nuns, and the apartment without indoor plumbing behind the Farmers Union store. I would never go back.

Park River, a town of 2,500 people in the Red River Valley, was only three hours east of Balta, but it was another country for a thirteen-year-old. We were moving from an insular community of two hundred German-Russian Catholics where the only Protestants in town were my dad and the depot agent to a place where the small Catholic congregation consisted of Polish and Bohemians, and where Scandinavian Lutherans predominated. From a school of fifty students, grades one through twelve, with teacher nuns, to a consolidated high school of two hundred. I had never seen a basketball or football game, nor participated in a choir or school band.

The possibilities were endless. I could start high school with a clean slate, erase the embarrassing Balta connection. I would shed the persona of the German-Russian hick. I studied to prove I could get good grades in a bigger school and joined every group from Future Homemakers of America to Science Club.

After freshman year, determined to dress as fashionably as the "in girls," I lied about my age and got a job at Smezak's Drive In. The Smezaks' best friends owned the local bakery. They observed my summer work and offered me a job, so in the fall I began my career at Jack and Judy's Bakery on Main Street. For the next three years, I got up at 6 a.m. to fill doughnuts with jelly and slice rounded loaves of bread to buy skirts and sweaters and blue suede shoes at the Johnson Store.

College was the only way out of smelling like a doughnut the rest of my life. Mom, determined too, added managing the Dairy Queen that summer to selling Stanley Home Products.

In the fall of 1957, with Mom's hard-earned stake, a tuition scholarship, and a job as student assistant in the University Business Office, I moved into Fulton Hall at the University of North Dakota in Grand Forks. Two occupations were acceptable for women in the late '50s—teaching and nursing. Except for confident, flamboyant Margie, who enrolled in fashion design and journalism, my high school friends chose teaching or nursing. Margie and I had co-edited the high school newspaper. I envied her daring, and enrolled safely in English Education.

Those first semesters in college, I attended Mass at the Newman Center and knelt there in prayer especially during final exams. My devotion waned after meeting Monte Phillips sophomore year. Christmas 1960, senior year, love trumped religion, and I abandoned my Catholicism without qualms to marry Monte.

The summer before the wedding, Mom made an appointment for me to see her parish priest. She liked Monte and had married a Protestant herself, but, perhaps, hoped to protect me from the challenges that entailed. I argued with her about seeing the priest. Then feigned indifference and trudged down the street to St. Mary's rectory.

Old Father O'Meara, of my high school years, had retired by this time. An unfamiliar young priest invited me into his study. I perched in a chair across from his desk, took the package of Kents out of my purse and lit up. He pushed an ash tray within my reach and proceeded to question me about Catholic doctrine. I actually hadn't thought about that. I remember my impatient, "Yes. Yes. Yes." I didn't disbelieve, I just wanted to get married. His last question concerned the Blessed Mother. I assured him I could revere her as devoutly as a Methodist. He shrugged and gave up. I left, smug as any twenty-year-old who knows everything.

Monte and I left North Dakota after he finished his master's degree in Engineering and taught for a year as an interim professor at the University of North Dakota. Anyone who was anyone growing up in North Dakota yearned to leave. My dream was West. "Our friends are all going to California," I whined when Monte accepted a teaching position in the College of Engineering at Ohio Northern State University. "Ohio? Who goes to Ohio?"

Mom rarely gave advice, nor discussed her own marriage, but she expressed strong opinions in this case. In the early 1940s, Dad wanted to leave North Dakota. His brother Peter and other unskilled, unschooled men were leaving the prairie for Seattle where jobs in the shipyards were profitable and plentiful because of the war. Mom's parents begged them not to take my sister and me away from them. Grandpa found Dad a job in Balta. Mom and Dad stayed in North Dakota.

"You go willingly wherever Monte needs to go for his work," Mom said, in an unusually demanding tone. "Your dad was never happy in his jobs. He couldn't earn a decent living in North Dakota. Staying was a mistake. I've always regretted it."

I did hear her advice, and I embraced every move in Monte's studies for a doctorate and his teaching career with enthusiasm for experiencing a new place and meeting new people. We lived in Ohio for a year, then briefly in New Mexico and Oklahoma. We settled in Champaign, Illinois, had three daughters, and bought a house in a neighborhood of young couples with kids.

The North Dakota taint clung to us. Over the years, the general perception of North Dakotans as ignorant often took me by surprise. I recalled that the relatives who visited us in the summer from East and West coasts brought a fascinating whiff of City along with a condescending attitude. The dollar bill Mom's California cousin Pius pressed into my hand as he patted me on the head and said good-bye was unexpected good fortune. Milky Way candy bars and Orange Crush cost a nickel. It galled mom —"galled," one of her words. We were interesting peasants.

I'd forgotten those childhood experiences, or maybe never ceased being naïve. I was taken aback the first time I heard, "I've never met anyone from *there* before." One Thanksgiving dinner, an Illinois friend, with her arm around my shoulder in a half hug, introduced me to her New Jersey mother with, "Niomi's from North Dakota, and she knows how to set a table as well as anyone." And Monte's office mate's wife, her Chicago-born nose tilted in disdain, once shriveled the dinner table conversation in our home with her response to a remark Monte made with, "That *must be* one of your quaint North Dakota sayings."

I didn't outgrow my sensitivity to being *from* North Dakota, but I was lonesome for family, especially my parents, and excited to move back home in 1970. With doctorate in hand, husband Monte took a position in the College of Engineering at the University of North Dakota. We moved back to Grand Forks with our three little girls. The boon for them and for us was residing only hours from our parents and our grandparents, all living at that time.

Mom had been the kind of long-distance Grandma who put contact paper on a box with a lid, filled it with old prom dresses, veiled hats, purses, and gloves and mailed it to our girls in Illinois for playing dress-up. She was the kind of Grandma who, in spite of modest means, put joy in little girls' winter days with a package of coloring books, crayons, paper dolls and scissors delivered to our door.

She and Dad visited us only once during our seven years in Illinois. They took the train from Fargo, North Dakota, to Champaign. Their suitcase went on to Chicago. For five days, Mom wore her travelling dress and a one-size-fits-all cotton flowered house coat with metal snaps down the front we purchased at Kmart.

Monte's pants and shirts fit Dad, but though Mom and I were the same height, she was plump, and I was stick thin. She didn't dwell on how she appeared to our friends and neighbors or let her wardrobe ruin the visit. On the 4th of July, she held court in our driveway, decorating wagons and tricycles with red, white, and blue streamers and blowing balloons. The neighbor kids vied for her attention and the gift of her joyous laugh.

Back in Grand Forks, Mom and Dad lived only an hour away. There Mom let Teri, Lisa, and Laura putter and paint in her basement ceramic shop. She played canasta with them and worked the jigsaw puzzle always set up on a card table in the living room during winter months. By the time they were teenagers, the bond was deep.

After oldest daughter Teri got her driver's license, the girls would announce they were going to see Grandma Betty and Grandpa Harold and take off on many a Sunday afternoon. Although often at odds with me in those testy years, they shared their high school experiences with Mom. She listened and laughed with them, enjoying their life so different from her own high school years. She didn't make judgments, just enjoyed their company and confidences.

She was the kind of mother who heard with relish the news of my life as faculty wife, school volunteer, School Board member, and then my adventure in returning to graduate school. By now she had a job at the local bank and her work life was interesting for me. And we read the same books and had similar interests in political issues. When I glimpsed her black Chevrolet in our driveway on my walk home from work at the University, I would run to get there before she decided to leave.

Christmas was Mom's favorite holiday. She prepared for weeks. She sewed or crocheted stockings and filled them for her grandkids and the neighbors' kids and her friends' grandkids. She came home from work and baked every evening.

When she and Dad arrived at our house Christmas Day, the holiday began. Dad would open the door and Mom would stagger in under her load of gifts and food. Even our Springer Spaniel went crazy barking to greet her. The girls rushed to the door to relieve her of the packages and get hugs.

Hugging Mom was like hugging a bag of marshmallows with a whiff of Este Lauder. Only 5'1" she was always on a diet of some sort. A cartoon on her refrigerator showed a humungous potato on a scale. The caption read: *If I call this a serving, it is a serving.*

Mom didn't set foot in my kitchen on those Christmas days except to put her boxes and pans of cookies and bars on the counter—fifteen different kinds the last year she joined us. Monte's mother set the table and then relaxed with a brandy and a cigarette. Grandma Bertsch, Mom's mother, the kitchen maven, put her apron on and bossed me through the turkey dinner. Mom settled down in the living room to play cards with her granddaughters.

In 1985, the breast cancer Mom had survived seven years before, metastasized to the bone and lung. On her sleepless nights, our last weeks together, in the quiet of the dark, Dad snoring down the hall, we sat at her kitchen table, cocooned. She didn't talk about her significant accomplishment in retiring as the first female officer of a local bank after years of picking potatoes, tending bar, and selling Stanley Home Products. She reminisced about her girlhood. And I was old enough to listen and to care. Like handmade lace tablecloths, we receive family stories with more appreciation in our middle age.

Mom had always been a vocal feminist, but practical in her causes, pleased with modest victories. When she finally became an officer in the local bank, she lobbied successfully for policy changes. The men would have to take turns working on Saturday mornings as well as the women. Women would be allowed to smoke at their desks just like the men. The latter amused me. Mom had never smoked.

"I never could learn to inhale," she giggled the day she tried smoking for the last time. We had drawn the drapes over the picture window facing the street in case a neighbor walked by and looked in. We filled the little pipe with the sage-like leaves a young bank colleague had passed to her in the parking lot after work. "It's good quality, Betty," she said, handing Mom a small brown paper bag. "It's supposed to help your nausea from the chemo."

Mom still couldn't inhale. I had smoked cigarettes for years, but was too cowardly to try marijuana. We laughed together, conspirators, enjoying the intimacy and secretiveness of it.

"I didn't smoke like some of my friends did when we were young," Mom said, "but I was rebellious, feisty. Always in trouble because I couldn't keep my mouth shut and didn't know 'my place.' It *wasn't* the good old days."

German-Russian men were unloving, or at least unaffectionate. Life was hard for women. "They had a baby every nine months and ten minutes," she said.

"At a meal a woman would have a baby in her lap, one in a high chair on one side, another on a stool at the other side. No man would so much as give the babies a cup of milk or a piece of bread—women's work," she said with a bitterness that took me by surprise.

"The women cooked three big meals a day for as many as fourteen people, baked bread, planted gardens, canned vegetables and meat, sewed everything but overalls, and pregnant or not, did the milking and took care of the pigs and chickens. Life was hell for women."

Mom's cousin Jenny once confided to her with awe that the Norwegian woman Jenny worked for didn't have to milk cows or work in the barn. And Jenny actually saw the woman's husband kiss her "in broad daylight."

Mom's Aunt Helen was unusually frank with her about sex for those times when kids often didn't know a new baby was expected until it arrived. Sex meant obligation and babies, Helen warned. She discussed her guilt in trying to prevent pregnancy and the subsequent irony of conceiving and birthing only one child—an embarrassment for her husband in a culture that measured manliness in number of offspring and especially male offspring.

Most of the men in the family didn't think education was necessary especially for girls, but Mom's dad did expect her to get good grades and to attend high school. She graduated from Alsen High School in 1937 at the head of her class.

Going to college was out of the question. There was no money. Like several of her female cousins, Mom went to work as a hired girl in Devils Lake. They cleaned and cooked, diapered babies, and looked forward to Saturday night dances and Sunday afternoons off. Mom was more fortunate than her cousins who were required to turn over all but fifty cents of their $2.50 a week to their fathers. Older siblings were expected to contribute to the family—there were seven or eight younger children at home to feed and clothe. Farming was a hard scrabble life. For the oldest girls in those families, a new baby was not an occasion for joy, only despair in greater obligation.

"Jenny and Margaret cried when they found out their mother was pregnant again. More work for them," Mom said, her voice breaking with remembered compassion for her cousin friends. The alternative for girls from those large families was marriage. Even at its worst, having a kitchen of their own was preferable to ending up as the family's maiden aunt, shunted from one household to another to help with the work.

The summer after high school graduation, Mom spent a weekend with her parents in Alsen where she ran into Harold Rohn, the older brother of her high school friend Eileen. He had just returned from his second winter in California in his new Model T. In a photo from the time, he leans nonchalantly against the hood of the car, his hat set jauntily back on his head, his long legs crossed—tall, handsome, sophisticated. Although she had been in and out of the Rohn house with Eileen, Mom was nine years younger, and Dad had never paid attention to her until then. Years later he told me, "Your mom was always laughing . . . full of fun."

He was a quiet, serious young man from a home with heavy silence, a dour atmosphere. His mother and dad rarely spoke to each other.

With the disapproval of both families, the Rohn Mennonites and the Bertsch Catholics, Betty Bertsch and Harold Rohn were married October 19, 1938. Mom was only nineteen; Dad was twenty-eight.

The summer of midnight table talk with Mom, her stories about her girlhood and her strong opinions about the role of German-Russian women, intrigued me. Until then I had ignored my ethnic background, not only incurious about it, but also reluctant to claim it.

Our family history is a familiar one in North Dakota. My ancestors were part of the German migration to Russia in the 18th century. Catherine the Great of Russia, herself a German, had offered free land, exemptions from service in the Russian army, religious freedom, local self-government, and tax exemptions. Germans could essentially remain German. Tsar Alexander II, who ruled from 1855 to 1881, curtailed the special privileges, ending self-government and the exemption from the Russian army. Then Tsar Alexander III came to the throne in 1881 with the objective of assimilating minority groups and placed all schools, government and parochial, under the control of the state. Russian became the language of instruction.

Thousands of Germans left. By 1920 nearly 70,000 Germans from Russia had found homes in North Dakota. Most of them were farmers and preferred the prairie to the bigger towns, establishing tightly-knit communities and homesteads alongside fellow Germans of similar religious beliefs. Unlike the Scandinavians who were almost all Lutheran, Germans were a diverse group—Catholic, Lutheran, Mennonite, and Baptist.

My maternal grandmother, Magdalena Senger Bertsch, was nine years old when she came to the United States with her parents, three brothers, and three sisters in 1909. After Mom died in 1985, I turned to Grandma and, ultimately, to the extended family for more of our story.

In 1987 Grandma and Great Aunt Helen, her widowed sister-in-law, lived across the hall from each other in Skyview Apartments in Devils Lake, North Dakota. Skyview, a subsidized housing complex, was home to forty-four elderly widows and four men, two of whom had cars. Downtown stores were within walking distance, but the day their Social Security checks arrived, some of the women, including Grandma and Aunt Helen, paid their men friends two dollars for rides to Kmart and the shopping center.

Grandma was 87 years old; Aunt Helen smug about being younger—four years. She danced with "the old geezers" at the American Legion Hall every chance she could and played bingo at Spirit Lake casino when she could "bum a ride." Grandma "tsked" about this "running around—at *her* age."

Grandma, on the other hand, held dominion over the kitchen affairs of Skyview which the residents referred to as "the high rise." A plaque honoring Grandma for eighteen years of service as a Senior Citizen volunteer hung on the wall next to a large crucifix above her chrome-legged dining table. She made plastic flower centerpieces for the tables in the dining room at Skyview, worked in the kitchen for Senior Meals two days a week, walked down the block to St. Joseph Catholic Church for daily Mass, and helped the priest distribute Communion to the "old people" next door in the nursing home on Wednesdays.

Photos of two local priests and Grandma's nephew, Monsignor Joseph Senger, occupied front row center on the top of her glass-front bookcase in her living/dining room. The family photos—daughters, granddaughters, great grandchildren—were displayed in generational order in the second and third rows.

The flowered velour sofa across the room from the small dining table displayed her handiwork: a brown, green, and orange afghan and three crochet-covered sofa pillows in various patterns and brazen colors, no two alike. Her eyes too weak for crocheting, she now made quilts in vibrant yellows, reds, and pinks for family and friends.

Grandma was a consummate realist. Soon after Mom died, Grandma paid for a casket and arranged for her own burial. Every Christmas she gifted the treasures from her cedar chest: crocheted lace tablecloths, doilies, potholders, and pillowcases with intricate crocheted edgings. She gave me the glass sugar bowl from "the old country" and a pair of candlesticks that had belonged to her mother, Frances Senger.

Grandma was bossy and opinionated, but she held her tongue in mixed company, always aware of her place among men. She gave me unconstrained advice in the kitchen, but I saw the inadvertent smile hovering at the edges of her thin lips when our family gathered. She assumed the submissive demeanor of a lifetime, tolerant and amused with men, smug in her conviction that it is women who preserve religion, nurture children, protect families, and orchestrate life.

Her apron was her armor. Christmas, Easter, illness, or death, you put your apron on and got to work. During the endless summer days when Mom was dying, Grandma cleaned the refrigerator, polished the stove, and made *kasnupla* and *kuchen*. After the funeral, she walked in the door, took her coat and her black purse to the bedroom, tied her apron around her ample waist, and plugged in the coffee pot.

I spent that winter of Sunday afternoons in 1987 at Skyview. I inhaled a mélange of cabbage and tomatoes, the essence of borscht, as I stepped out of the elevator on the 3rd floor. The women at Skyview cooked and baked with a competition as keen as the skill they brought to the card table set up in the sitting area next to the elevator. They taped towels over the sensitive smoke detectors to prevent the annoying beeps when pie juices ran over in the oven.

I settled into a chair at Grandma's table, the story of German-Russian women my obsession and a palliative for my grief over Mom's death. My own year of magical thinking. I used a tape recorder to capture the stories. Aunt Helen often joined us.

Aunt Helen brought my mom to life. She laughed with Mom's spontaneity and delight. She bubbled joy no matter that her life had never been easy. She had always worked for minimum wage. She had no income but minimum Social Security. She always made me laugh.

Sensible, organized, practical Grandma scoffed at what she called Helen's scatter-brain. With a streak of jealousy, Grandma tried to keep me to herself. Some Sundays she forgot to tell Helen when I planned to arrive.

On the audio tape, you can hear the door into the small apartment open, and faint in the background, "Oh, Niomi. I didn't know you were here." A chair scrapes the floor. Petite Aunt Helen in her pink polyester slacks and matching pink sweatshirt joined the conversation. She was a contrast to my stout grandma in her flowered house dress and flowered apron with the bias tape trim. And they were unalike in responses to my questions. Grandma rarely spoke without thoughtful consideration. Aunt Helen made giggling, snide asides and corrected Grandma with, "Well, this is my two cents."

The room became peopled with children, girls, women, weaving back and forth from Russia to North Dakota.

Grandma remembered her own widowed grandmother, who managed a winery and farm, in the Kutschurgan, and gave her a shawl the last day. The family gathered at the farm the day Grandma's family left for Odessa. *Grossmutter* offered three shawls—gray, green, and black. "Yah und I got the black because I was the youngest gel and had last choice," she said.

I laughed. "Isn't that a typical kid? Your grandmother is saying goodbye to her son and his family. They are parting forever. They will never see each other again. And you remember it because you were jealous about the shawl."

Grandma pushed her chair away from the table, left the room, and returned with the fringed, black shawl. She wrapped it around my shoulders. She scolded, "I remember more." She shook her head at my scoffing at her faulty memory. "Just off the ship . . . the hotel in New York where the boys (her three brothers) couldn't figure how to work the faucets on the sink. Then they thought the toothpicks on the table in the restaurant were something to eat." Grandma was nine years old.

"We came over in August, 1909," she said. "The folks didn't want the boys to serve in the Russian army. We first came to Harvey where the folks had relatives.

"*Grossmutter* stayed back and two of my mother's brothers stayed. They lost everything. *Grossmutter* died on the way . . . oh, what's that? Ya, Siberia. One uncle died before that happened. Ya, I remember the day they drove us to Odessa to the train. All the neighbors came to say good-bye. Six families left for Odessa that day. Two of my dad's brothers and others.

"My sister Kathryn had glaucoma and had to have surgery before we could leave Odessa. We had to take a freight ship so it was a long trip. It was the last ship before winter set in." (It is unlikely that the problem was glaucoma, but that was Grandma's understanding.)

"On the ship, the older boys weren't with the family. The girls and youngest kids, like my brother Joe—he was not quite two years older than me (sic)—were with the parents. Joe and I were the only ones who didn't get sick on the ship. We carried food and water to them."

Grandma and I moved on to talk about life in North Dakota. She tried to elude some of my questions. I wanted to know, for example, if German-Russian attitudes toward education were as different from other North Dakota settlers as I had been told and read.

According to North Dakota historian Handy-Marchello, four years of high school were not available at some German-Russian schools until the late 1930s; by comparison, communities with predominantly Norwegian populations had four-year high schools ten years earlier.

Grandma wanted to create her own story, so I learned to pose questions that wouldn't sound like judgments. *Who went to school in your family? Tell me about your older sister, Julia. Julia preferred to speak German, never spoke English very well. How did you learn? You only went to school through 4th grade. How did you learn to write?*

Grandma's answers were restrained. She paused often and put me off impatiently with "That's just the way it was" or "That was the style."

"I worked in the fields with my brother Joe when I was nine years old," she said. "We were poor.

"My older brothers and sisters worked out. They brought home everything they earned. Every family did it that way."

She worked with Joe and their dad plowing, planting, haying and harvesting. In between there were chickens to feed, cows to milk, gardening, canning, washing, and ironing.

"Schooling was not for girls in those days," she said defensively, aware of my passion for education. "Girls were supposed to be able to cook and sew and keep house." Her older brothers and sisters never attended school. She attended in the winter for a couple months after fall harvest and before spring work. "If the crops were out, or the crops were in, and the horses could get through the snow."

Aunt Helen was delightfully unrestrained. Her brown eyes sparkled with mischief and the pure fun of telling me stories. A spitfire, she interrupted, impatient with Grandma's studied, cautious responses to my questions.

"Women were slaves. They had to get up early in the morning, carry in the water, then carry out the water. Raise the kids. Work like a man. All the old German ladies have arthritis in their arms now . . . Sure and the Norwegians don't. My neighbor, old Mrs. Olson, doesn't have an ache in her body," she adds, indignant with the old Catholic/Lutheran, Norwegian/German antipathy.

I laughed with enjoyment in her candor and her spontaneous opinions. Unlike Grandma, she didn't sift her thoughts for politically correct or socially acceptable expressions. She wasn't concerned with creating a pleasant history.

Aunt Helen didn't qualify her opinions about the German-Russian attitude toward education, and she offered opinions about the differences between Germans and Scandinavians without my prompting. "The Norwegians seen to it that their kids got an education," she said, drumming her pink, polished nails on the table.

"They went from day one. My oldest sister didn't get to go to school at all. The boys did—when the weather was good and there was no work to do. Your grandpa got the most. He finished 8th grade. He even taught in that country school near Orrin one winter when they needed a teacher . . . I had to milk three cows before I went to school. The Norwegian girls didn't have to work outside. Pa wouldn't even let us speak English at home."

Without a pause she rants, "My dad was a real son-of-a-bitch. 'Get out in the kitchen. Mind your own business,' he'd tell me when the families were together. Men always in one room. Women in another. I was so glad to get away from home. I didn't want to stay on the farm and have twelve kids. I was never so happy as when I got married—lots of girls got married to get away, to have it easier."

"That was just expected," Grandma interrupted, impatient, anxious to shut her up. "Getting married and having your own home was just expected."

After Helen left, Grandma shook her head in disgust and amended the story. "Her dad was just loud talking (talked loud). *She* had to work *so* hard. That was nothing new. Everybody worked hard. Our boys (Sengers) didn't milk either. That was a woman's job."

Grandma was eighteen years old when she married Anton Bertsch, Aunt Helen's brother who had graduated from 8th grade and taught briefly in a country school. Anton was a worldly young man by my grandmother Magdalena's standards He had ventured from Orrin to Grand Forks to work on the railroad. "He mixed with all kinds and learned English," she told me with pride.

For two years after their marriage, Magdalena and Anton lived down the street from her parents in the Catholic German-Russian community of Orrin where they had grown up and where my mother, Elizabeth, and her sister, Frances, were born. Then Grandpa got a job with the Soo Line Railroad, and they moved to Harlow. "There were Americans there," Grandma said. "Mostly Norwegians. I went a lot of time to the store and I couldn't ask for what I needed. I didn't know English." She was 25 years old.

"How did you learn English?" I asked.

"You can learn by yourself. I learned from the kids—your ma and Frances. Your ma started school there. She brought her books home. I studied like a little kid to learn English."

From Harlow they moved to Alsen, a community of Norwegians and German-Russian Mennonites in Cavalier County. "Mixed people, but really nice people," Grandma said. "You get different ideas when you live with different people. In Orrin you were all the same. It wasn't easy when you moved away, but we got along just fine."

In Alsen Grandma's niece Vernice joined the family. Vernice's mother, Grandma's youngest sister, had died in childbirth. Six children from that family made homes with Aunts and Uncles. "Vernice was our daughter from age four," Grandma says. "It was the Lord's way . . . my having only two girls. And a boy—miscarried. I could care for others."

"What about those big families?" I asked. "Were women happy about it?"

"That was the style," Grandma said. And then, sensing my disdain, she chuckled. "Norwegians had big families too."

"Did women talk about it?"

"Well, talking didn't help," she laughed and I joined her in this irony.

I tried to probe the family problem with alcoholism my mom had alluded to. "Some of the Senger boys drank too much," Aunt Helen admitted, "and so did your grandpa and two of my other brothers (Bertsch)."

Then she chuckled with the warm memory of my grandpa's humor and his generosity. "When your grandpa had a few too many, he'd say, 'I'm gonna get hell when I get home.' He'd give his shirt away when he was drunk."

Grandma wasn't interested in discussing the alcoholism. I tried to approach the subject by focusing on her. "It must have been hard for you. It must have been a struggle to manage with Grandpa's drinking." I had adored him, but he had died sixteen years before, so I assumed no disloyalty.

But Grandma was smart enough to see beyond the ruse of my pop psychology. "That's just the way it was," she repeated, twisting her thin gold wedding band. End of discussion.

My quest for affirmation and the truths of Mom's story led me from Grandma and Aunt Helen to the first generation of my German-Russian family born in the United States—Mom's cousins.

I wrote to three of them from three different families. They were in their late 60s then (1987-1988) and willing, even eager, to answer my questions. It occurred to me that no one had ever asked them about their growing up years. In every letter of response, grueling, unrelenting physical labor dominated their recollections. Cousin Jenny "escaped" to town to work as a hired girl, but her father "came in from the farm" on Saturdays to collect her paycheck. She turned it over to him, as he had turned his over to his father when he came from Russia as a boy.

Cousin Jenny wrote, "We had to work out and earn money to care for ourselves. And I was glad to leave home. We were so hard up then, so many kids to feed and dress. But your mother Elizabeth and her sister Frances had it a lot better. At least I thought they did. There were only two kids in the family. They lived in town and graduated from high school. None of us ever got to go to high school. I didn't even dream of it. Women worked so hard, that's all they knew was work."

Mom's cousin, Tom Senger, lived in rural Devils Lake. He wrote and reminded me that he and Mom grew up in "the dirty Thirties."

"I quit high school in the second year thinking it was the thing to do, get work of some kind and try to make a few dollars. Everybody back then seemed to work hard. The folks seemed to think that learning how to work was more important than school."

Another cousin, Frances Bertsch Fettig, went to live with Aunt Julia (Senger Bertsch) after her mother died and she and her siblings were divided among the family. Julia, who hadn't attended school herself after coming here from Russia, and always preferred speaking German, believed school was unnecessary for girls. "Girls needed to learn housework, so on washdays and canning days and during the harvest I had to stay home," Frances said. It was 1930. She was thirteen years old.

Mom's end of life reminiscences, her views of girlhood and womanhood in the German-Russian culture were shared by her family contemporaries. Not much had changed for this first generation born in the United States.

Then in 2002 cousin Monsignor Joseph Senger, the priest whose photograph sat center front on Grandma's display of family photographs, produced a video documentary about the German-Russian immigration to North Dakota. I was eager to see the film and learn more about our shared heritage. I was also proud of Father Joe for his prominent role in documenting and preserving the history of the German-Russians. I put the video in the VCR with great anticipation and enjoyed the opening scenes of North Dakota summer—prairie sky and golden fields. North Dakota at its best. The video was a reflection on rural life, as experienced by Father Joe and his family in Orrin, North Dakota. He referred to the Senger family's life in the Homeland (Russia), the beautiful crops in the Ukraine, the vineyards, and the villages in the Kutschurgan where our families lived for over a hundred years before immigrating to the United States.

The photography is beautiful—a pastoral setting, the family working together in the golden fields under the endless prairie sky; the background music, a soothing accompaniment to the sunrise, sunset, and clouds hovering in the blue sky, over the farm and over the tree-lined path to Orrin's Catholic Church. Nostalgic. Bucolic.

"We had a wonderful time on the farm," Father Joe says, recalling the smell of the clover and the fresh earth after plowing.

He describes his dad as gregarious. His mother as "a mild person."

"She had some difficulty after her second child . . . she had seven others subsequently.

"We had to help her a lot, even with cooking. She couldn't lift things. She was kind of feeble. A delicate person." He pauses, seems to consider a most important aspect of his mother's personality. "She was a mild, pleasant, pious woman. She went to Mass every day."

I watched the video, waiting for more. Some substance. Something more real. Not just nostalgia. Where were his sisters in this beautiful life on the farm? I remember three of his sisters hoeing in the garden, bringing eggs in from the chicken house, peeling buckets of potatoes in the kitchen. I spent many summer afternoons at that farm home with Grandma. Those girls must have been teenagers. I was seven or eight years old. I could tell by their laughter and conversation, English interspersed with German, that they enjoyed my grandma. Many years later, one of the three sisters told me that Grandma taught them to cook.

I wrote to Father Joe. "What about the women? You didn't give a picture of women's work and their lives." I posed a barrage of questions relating my conversations with my mother and other cousins. Their memories didn't correspond with the life in Father Joe's video, although they were contemporaries, the first generation of our German-Russian family born in the United States.

Father Joe acknowledged that life was hard for women. "But everyone worked hard," he wrote. "Those marriages were partnerships."

Marriage as a partnership wasn't something I had heard from the women I talked to. I resented his sentimentality and his priestly, superior male attitude.

I could hear my mom's voice with her hearty, good-humored laugh. "Father Joe's truth doesn't bear any resemblance to mine."

"It wasn't the good old days," echoed in my heart. I fumed about the film and Father Joe's story, especially to my ex-Catholic and anti-Catholic friends. Over the years, I had passed from embarrassment about growing up German-Russian in Balta to disdain for the place and for the Catholic Church.

But the heritage hovered. I needed to go to Balta to consider my roots.

References

Everett C. Albers and D. Jerome Tweton, editors
The Way It Was: The North Dakota Frontier Experience: Germans from Russia Settlers, Grass Roots Press, 1999.

Handy-Marchello, B. *Heritage Review,* May 1987.

Voeller, J. "The Origin of the German-Russian People and their Role in North Dakota," Master's Thesis. Grand Forks: University of North Dakota, 1940.

In 1940 Joseph Voeller, Superintendent of Schools of Pierce County and a German-Russian descendent, called the German-Russians, "the problem people in North Dakota." He described them as "backward, socially and emotionally retarded" and he wanted them "to appreciate education." He denigrated their clannishness and their absorption with farming at the expense of their children's education. Voeller found that in rural areas some of the first generation born in the U.S were still speaking German exclusively in their homes. In Pierce County and in other counties where German-Russians predominated, it was difficult to get them to send their children to school and keep them there.

Information from my grandmother, Magdalena Senger Bertsch and from Great Aunt Helen Bertsch Lalie was tape recorded in 1987. The tapes are in my possession. Information from Mother's cousins, Jenny Senger Bertsch, Tom Senger, and Frances Bertsch Fettig is from letters.

2

BACK TO BALTA

October, 2007

After all these years, my cousin Vernice, who lived with my grandparents, is my lone connection to Balta. Her husband, Nick Axtmann, looms large in my childhood memory. His boisterous loudness and swaggering confidence intimidated me. He seemed big. He was muscular with the strength born of strenuous farm work. He strutted. After I grew up, I realized he was only 5′3″ and, except for a paunch, not a large man at all.

As the years went by and his body bent and thinned with age and arthritis, his know-it-all bluster diminished. He relished reminiscing about "getting together" with my mom and dad and "the olden times"—always the good times. His affection for Mom was evident in his recounting their laughter and their arguments. As a child, overhearing their arguing, my stomach churned. I thought he was being mean to my mom. And I just knew she was smarter than he. Now it occurred to me that perhaps the arguing was enjoyable for her. He was an intelligent person and, perhaps, he was the only man she knew who would consider her worthy or even equal to debate.

Vernice had been raised like a sister to my mom. She was three years old when her own mother died in childbirth. Her dad, a black sheep, a con man, couldn't hold a job and drank too much, according to family lore. When he couldn't cope, his sisters and brothers divided the six kids. My grandparents, Magdalena and Anton Bertsch, took Vernice.

"Marie (the newborn) and I were the lucky ones," Vernice told me. "Aunt Julia took Marie for her own. Aunt Lena and Uncle Anton took me and loved me just like their own girls, your ma and Frances. The others (four older siblings) were farmed out. Those relatives all had big families of their own. Those kids were shuttled from place to place . . . never had a home."

After my mom and my grandmother died, I often visited Vernice and Nick in Rugby where they had moved after retiring from their Balta farm.

When Nick was in his eighties, his shoulders rounded. All his edges smoothed. He took me by surprise when I said good-bye at the end of one afternoon visit. "Thanks for stopping by. Spend the night some time. You're always welcome here." The child in me was moved to tears.

Nick and Mom had sparred about political parties and social issues decades before, and he still had keen interest in politics and government. He talked about crop prices and the state of farming in North Dakota. He watched FOX news between Vernice's soap operas, and he kept up with world affairs.

He talked about a grandson in Iraq with resignation. He raised his voice about women in the army, "No place for women." He was incensed by "the whining" of the families of Iraq and Afghanistan servicemen. The depth of his patriotism took me aback. He still believed in the ultimate wisdom of our leaders and their decisions.

The war in Iraq led him to reminisce about WWII and a hint of dissatisfaction with the church. He noted bitterly the disadvantage of having only one brother in his family of eight. "Every family was expected," he said, "to give two children to the church—a priest and a nun.

"My brother Joe got chosen for priest. He went off to seminary and I had to stay on the farm. I couldn't be drafted. One son from each family had to be exempt from the draft to keep the farms going. The country needed the food. I wanted to run away and enlist, but I didn't dare."

After all these years—four wars since WWII—this disappointment rankled.

In our last conversations, Nick's reminiscent stories changed. He focused on himself. Without provocation he offered, "My dad was a hard man. He only went to 4th grade in "the old country" (Russia). They (German-Russians) weren't much for education. Kids had to help with the farm work. It wasn't much different here (in Balta) than in "the old country." Spring and fall farm work. School only in winter. I couldn't go to high school."

Layers of his life fell away in his telling. I began to see the boy who learned to be tough and hard even if it wasn't in his nature. A young man who had to follow the example and live up to the expectations of his dad and the German-Russian culture on the harsh Dakota prairie, only one generation removed from "the old country."

My view of him changed dramatically from that narrow window of childhood. It had taken decades, but I was grateful both of us had lived long enough for my understanding. And Nick echoed and confirmed my mother's observations of life for the first generation of German-Russians born in the United States. This though, a glimpse of the male point of view.

Over the years I had worked at kindling Vernice's memories of the past, but she was not reflective, and she couldn't break the habit of secrets even when the people involved were dead. I was still trying to discover some truth about Grandpa's excessive drinking, for example. We would call him an alcoholic today.

"How did Grandpa's drinking affect you and Mom? Was Grandma bossy because he drank, or did he drink because she was so bossy?" I would prime with a smile. She would pause, twisting her gnarled, arthritic hands in her lap, and shelve that topic with the same old, "all the German men drank a lot in those days."

"Well, what about that? What in the culture and their life led to excessive drinking?" I prodded. If she had an opinion, she wouldn't voice it.

Once in a while she would offer me a sketchy, mundane anecdote from the past, but then turn to look across the room at Nick, waiting for him to concur? Elaborate? Approve? She had always deferred to him, so unlike my mother who chaffed at deference to men.

In the late 1980s, Vernice developed Parkinson's disease. The symptoms progressed slowly but relentlessly year after year. Nick would lift himself up from his La-Z-Boy recliner to pour coffee, and he served the *kuchen* he had helped her make for my visit.

She had to quit driving, so he took her to her Altar Society meetings and to the beauty shop for her weekly hair appointment. He sat in the car, listening to radio, waiting patiently to take her home.

He was pleased in my interest in seeing Balta, since I hadn't been there in over fifty years. "Vernice and I will be your tour guides," he suggested with a chuckle, when Monte and I stopped by that October day in 2007.

Sensing my excitement in the short drive from Rugby, he said, "*You* are going to be disappointed, Niomi."

The sixteen miles on highway #3 south from Rugby to Balta were paved. The drive I remembered was a long, pot-holed one on a gravel road, an expedition not taken lightly, especially in the spring when country roads turned to muck, or in the winter, when plows made a corridor through the snow scarcely wide enough for two cars to pass.

I recalled one blustery winter Sunday afternoon, after weeks of being snowed in, Dad and Grandpa decided they had to see Roy Rogers and Trigger at the Rugby Lyric Theatre matinee. Grandma said *she* had better sense than to risk making that drive in a snow storm. Mom agreed with her. "Reckless to go in this weather," she said.

I couldn't resist the break from boredom and sat in the back seat, mouth clamped shut, the air thick with fear as the old Hudson lurched and bucked with Dad's efforts to keep it in the track and out of the snow banks.

The history of the late 1940s bears out my recollections of ten-foot-high snow banks on each side of the car. The snowstorms were so severe in 1947-1948, that the National Guard was called to plow the town out.

This autumn day we drove those sixteen miles in a flash. Leaning over the front seat to get a better view of the farms and crops on both sides of the road, I wrote the story of this return in my head. I anticipated my emotion, immersed in nostalgia, washed over with love of prairie and home. I anticipated the hill just outside of town where we picked crocuses in the spring. I could see us, my best friend Antoinette and me, bare-legged, hair blowing in the warm wind, running, free, free of wool scarves and heavy coats, picking crocuses to put in the baskets we would carry in the processional for the May Crowning at Our Lady of Mount Carmel Church.

But the town had blended into the barren browned autumn prairie. There was no edge. There was no hill just outside of the first cluster of houses. Were we so desperate for elevation?

Nothing was recognizable. Vernice pointed out Grandma and Grandpa's house—a small square building with peeling paint on the corner of a barren piece of ground. In my memory, the house Grandpa and his friends built was large and spacious. Grandpa let me have a hammer and nails to pound into the lath he was nailing to wall studs in preparation for plaster. The men helping him scoffed at his letting "the gel" use a hammer. "She's just going to get in the way."

The entry way, big kitchen, pantry, and dining room of Grandma and Grandpa's house were separated from the living room by an arched doorway, a niche on each side of the arch for the statues—the Blessed Mother and St. Anthony. Crocheted doilies adorned the backs and arms of the maroon frieze sofa and matching chair in the living room. I often found

Grandma at her sewing machine in the spare bedroom where I'd stand on one foot, then another, impatient for her to finish measuring the hem for my dress, whining about the pins sticking my bare legs.

My friends and I played hide and seek midst the rows of corn in the vegetable garden at the back of the house. Grandma tended brick-enclosed flower beds of peonies and gladiolas in the spacious front yard and a strawberry patch next to the chicken shed in the back.

Mom and Dad, little sister Vickie, and I lived four blocks away in an apartment behind the Farmers Union Oil Company garage and store on Main Street. We had a pump at the kitchen sink and an outhouse, so Grandma and Grandpa's house with its indoor plumbing was luxurious by comparison.

It was a warm house. Bread and *kuchen* baking. *Kasnupla* in a white and green casserole wrapped in a white dish towel, knotted into a handle for my small hands to carry home. It was warm with the comfort of Grandma at the kitchen counter in her apron and Grandpa at the table reading the newspaper or working a crossword puzzle. He drew cartoon pictures to amuse me at that table, and I plunked my math books there for his help.

I remember gardens—flower gardens and vegetable gardens—in orderly squares behind every fence next to every white house. Gates opened into both front and back yards, wooden slat sidewalks leading from back doors to shed and gardens. Next door to Grandma, old Mrs. Fettig, her babushka tied under her chin, swept her sidewalk every morning, greeting passersby in German.

Now, fences were falling down around unpainted buildings. Old cars, discarded washing machines, and trash were partially buried among waist-high weeds at back doors.

Monte asked if he should take photos. I barked, "No." I seemed to own the town's embarrassing decline. Even the brick bank building next door to the Farmers Union was gone.

In the late 1940s, that old brick bank building had been converted into a charming apartment where Marilyn Kjonaas, my exotic, tall, blond, 5th grade friend lived. Marilyn was the only transplant to the town I ever knew. That year, I abandoned my best friend Antoinette for Marilyn whenever I could. Marilyn's dad managed one of the grain elevators, and her mother was a nurse who drove to Rugby every day to work at the hospital. My mom sometimes worked as a substitute postmaster, picked potatoes in the fall, and even tended bar on Saturday dance nights, but I didn't know another woman who worked outside her home, especially one who had a profession. When the Kjonaases didn't want to leave Marilyn alone, they invited me to spend the night. I was self-conscious about my faded pajamas and sagging elastic underpants, but couldn't resist the experiences so different from any I knew.

On one of those slumber party nights, Marilyn and I cut our bangs with a fingernail scissors, sitting on the floor in front of the full-length mirror in the bank vault. Her mother had turned the vault into a walk-in closet. I had never seen so many clothes.

Another world opened up to my ten-year-old self at their dinner table where I tasted my first Italian spaghetti served with garlic bread, and where their dinner-time world reached outside of Pierce County. Their conversation focused on the news from Marilyn's brother Bob serving in the army under General McArthur in Korea. I listened to their impassioned conversation about the tragedy in President Truman's dismissal of the General. An opinion quite different from the one I heard at home.

Marilyn confided that her mother hated Balta. When the school year ended, they left.

In those days, Andy's tavern and dance hall occupied the first building in the block across the street from Marilyn's bank home. Grandpa sat at Andy's bar too often, and treated his friends too generously, especially on the Soo Line Railroad's payday. On those occasions, Grandma sent me to stand in the doorway, where the cool dark air and not unpleasant smell of beer met me, and where I called to Andy behind the bar to send my grandpa home. I would hold his hand walking down the street. He would stumble up the steps. We would both brace for the harangue. Grandma would push him from the kitchen through the living room to the bedroom, scolding in German all the way. One swipe of his meaty, big hand would have taken her out, but he went meekly. And I blamed her. Mean.

Across the street from the Farmers Union where my dad worked delivering gas to the farmers and greasing their cars and trucks, a grocery store housed the Post Office and creamery. Another tavern anchored that block. Next, Johnny Schaan's Standard Oil Service Station and Antoinette's dad's hardware store. Both gone. Two decrepit buildings remained in those four blocks.

Maybe the mercantile part of Main Street had never been more than two blocks long?

The tour of Balta took about ten minutes. And Nick wasn't wrong. I was disheartened. How naïve. Small towns were dying all over the prairie; how could I imagine Balta would be immune from the death?

One thing hadn't changed. Our Lady of Mount Carmel Catholic Church still stood at the end of the street where I remembered it, but the priest's house was gone. Antoinette's house stood alone on the block across from the church—abandoned. I had loved that house. I saw myself opening the gate and walking around to the side yard where we played croquet. Antoinette and her sister Jo Clare had a spacious bedroom with a carpet and twin beds on the second floor under the eaves. Someday I thought then, I will not live in an apartment. I will live in a real house with a bedroom like this.

Antoinette embodied my worst sins. Obeying the other nine commandments wasn't all that difficult. I can still recite them from the Baltimore Catechism today, and still stumble over the "coveting" one. I could cover the "Thou shalt not bear false witness," with a little fibbing when necessary, but the "Thou shalt not covet they neighbor's goods" was, and is, a challenge.

Coveting was born in me young. Antoinette was my bosom buddy (my bff or soul mate in today's vernacular). We had twin imaginations. There weren't enough hours in any day for our imaginative wanderings. But I coveted her goods—her big house, her bedroom under the eaves of their second floor, her yard with the big vegetable and flower gardens and a lawn that invited croquet.

Then there was a baby brother. My stomach lurched the day she told me with the drama of a "big secret" that her mother was going to have a baby. I wanted everything she had including another sibling though I paid scant attention to my own younger sister. Antoinette had Jo Clare and I had Vickie, so we were even. Now she would have another, and worst of all, it turned out to be a brother.

Vernice asked if I would like to go into the church. We walked up the broad front steps. I hesitated, then put my hand on the latch. The door was unlocked. A deserted town with an open church.

I stood at the back of the church between the marble holy water fonts. I saw it peopled. Black babushka-clad old women in the left back pews. Younger women with colorful head scarves in front of them with the babies and small children. Black-veiled Nuns, guardians of our behavior, in row ten. Children in order of grade in front of the nuns. Twitching or whispering would bring one of them to your place and to public humiliation during the hour-long mass with a sermon in both English and German. Sister Mary Dominic, Sister Mary Ellen, Sister Mary Anastasia's eyes were on you. Assume a pious demeanor, hands folded, eyes down when returning from Communion. Don't fidget or whisper. Men and boys on the right side of the church. I saw Mom's friend Clara come in with her husband Joe and sit on the men's side, one small defiant act. Visitors, extended family, or young people returning home for the holidays, sometimes dared to flaunt the tradition as well. In the back pews, the old women in their black shawls looked up from their missals and shook their heads in disdain.

Our Lady of Mount Carmel is a church in the style of European Cathedrals. Stained glass windows, two side altars, life-sized statues, an ornate front altar set into a large niche reached by a bank of steps, separating, distancing the priest and the sacrifice of the Mass from the congregation.

The rounded, vaulted ceiling was still blue with stars, the marble front altar set in an alcove facing a magnificent life-sized crucifix, with angels, bigger than life, hovering on each side above the crucifix. The Blessed Mother still resided life-sized on one of the side altars facing girls and women. We prayed to her, our conduit to her son.

A guest book rested on a podium near the holy water fonts just inside the door at the back of the church. There I found the name—Antoinette Klevgard (nee Schmaltz), my childhood friend. Grandma and Grandpa, Mom and Dad, even my sister, were gone. Antoinette and I had been simpatico children. I needed her to affirm my memories of this place. I needed to find her.

3

FINDING ANTOINETTE

How do I find Antoinette?

I had never been interested in exploring the internet to locate people from the past, but I recalled seeing requests for names and information from the Germans from Russia Heritage Collection (GRHC) website. This is a privately funded, specialized archive located at North Dakota State University in Fargo, North Dakota. Through Director and Bibliographer Michael M. Miller and his staff, Germans from Russia have access to one of the most comprehensive collections of German-Russian resources in the world.

In October, 2007, I emailed Michael Miller at GRHC to ask if anyone could put me in contact with Antoinette Schmaltz Klevgard. I noted our grade school connection in Balta, North Dakota, during the 1940s and 1950s and Our Lady of Mount Carmel Catholic Church in Balta.

Within days I began to receive emails with advice on conducting an internet search as well as information about Antoinette. In trying to find her, I discovered the anticipation and then the enjoyment of opening my email to connect with strangers.

October 23, 2007
Hi—Through Yahoo People search, there was a Duane Klevgard listed at 3008 Silva Lane, Richmond, VA. If not him, perhaps a parent or relative? I typed name in and used North Dakota.
OR—Ask the pastor/people of the church. Someone must have spoken with them. You know how small towns are ☺.
Good luck,
Wanda
Former North Dakotan

October 24, 2007
Hi Niomi—
When I read the name, I thought I would see what I could do to help. With that name, I have to believe you are the daughter of Harold and Betty Rohn. I don't recall having met you, but I come from Alsen, ND, home of the Rohn family. My aunt was married to your uncle. I have been looking into the origins of many of the families from the Alsen/Munich areas.
Anyhow, after a couple of minutes on the internet, I came up with the information below. Hopefully it is still current. Having had a computer for only a year, I am still a novice, but I've had enough curiosity about some people that have passed through my life that I've made a few web searches. I just type "find a person" in Google and check out the websites.
Best regards—Ronald

October 31, 2007
Niomi,
I am a member of GRHC. My sister-in-law grew up near Balta, and she and her family belong to Mount Carmel Church. I checked with her and she knew Antoinette. In fact, she was Antoinette's confirmation sponsor. Antoinette's address is as follows:
Antoinette Schmaltz Klevgard
3008 Silva Lane
Richmond, VA

Don Schaan, whose great-grandparents homesteaded near Balta, not only responded to my request for information about Antoinette, but also offered to send me a history of Balta written by his dad, Frank Schaan, for the 75th Jubilee Celebration and All School Reunion in 1987. Don, an artist, has lived in California for thirty years, but his mother lives in Rugby, North Dakota, he has extended family in North Dakota, and he returns at least once a year.

October 31, 2007
From: Don Schaan
If you want to reconnect to Balta, you came to the right person. I have a real affinity towards Balta and the state of North Dakota. I categorize the art I have worked at over the years as American Western and Balta fits into that.

With the address provided through GRHC by my German-Russian correspondents, I wrote to Antoinette and she responded via email:

November 7, 2007
From: Antoinette Schmaltz Klevgard
Subject: Childhood memories–oh my!
Dear Niomi,
What a great surprise getting your letter . . .
Man, did you open a door to a room full of memories! Remember our bicycle club? We would sit on the slope by the side of the church and have our meetings. In the winter, we would play on top of the snow bank next to our hardware store. We used blocks of snow to divide the bank into rooms to play house. Remember when we played house and wore our Grandmothers' dresses and shoes? And traipse up and down the alley from my house to your playhouse that your Grandpa built for you? Talk about envy! And you had paper dolls! My dad thought they were a waste of money and wouldn't let me have them☹. I remember you had a black

baby doll. You were way ahead of your time ☺. And we used to make sugar bread at your house. I thought that was pure delight! And before we moved to Grandpa Schmaltz's house, we used to play in the garage/barn behind the hardware store. And this is only the beginning. Will get back to you soon.
P.S. And I do like it that you call me Antoinette. Duane (Antoinette's husband) and friends and family since Balta have known me as Toni. So only my cousins in ND call me Antoinette.
Antoinette/Toni

I do remember playing dress up. But the clothes and shoes, in my case, came from my fashionable Aunt Fran who lived in Seattle and worked at the Bon Marche'. When hem lengths moved up or down or platform shoes were replaced by sleek pumps, Aunt Fran sent boxes of her discarded skirts and dresses and high-heeled shoes with purses to match.

The clothes were Antoinette's and my costumes. We kindled each other's imaginations, one idea sparking another. Our make-believe worlds were boundless, the themes for our theater gleaned from the lives of the saints and books like *Heidi* and the latest movie heroines. Our hours together were never enough. We couldn't conclude the evolving drama in one afternoon. The story had to be continued, the characters picked up on the next precious play date.

I always preferred to play at her house—the apartment above her dad's hardware store and then the place she refers to as Grandpa Schmaltz' house. I was four or five years old the first time I played with her in the apartment above the hardware store, just down the block and across the street from my apartment in the back of the Farmers Union. I remember walking up the stairs and the door at the top of the stairs opening directly into the living room.

"That's Mary," Antoinette pointed, "our hired girl." Antoinette's mom and Mary were taking a break from their work, sitting amidst big, fluffy pillows on a cream-colored sofa, their legs tucked under them, drinking coffee and smoking cigarettes. I stared, fascinated. The only woman I knew who smoked was my city aunt, Fran. And a hired girl? My cousin Vernice on the farm had a hired girl, but a town woman?

The room wasn't tidy like our living room or Grandma's living room. Books and magazines, knitting needles and yarn covered the tops of the big, round coffee table and the end tables. Baskets of fabric and sewing projects were scattered haphazardly everywhere. So much to observe! The heavy fabric on brass rings separating the living room from the master bedroom intrigued me. No door. Antoinette called it a drape. I only knew curtains, the organdy white ruffled kind that Mom and Grandma dipped in starch and stretched over pins on a rack to dry after spring cleaning. Antoinette's mom created a home different from any I knew. Interesting. Messy. Cozy. And by the time I overhead Grandma scoff about Eloie Schmaltz' lack of housekeeping skills, I'd made up my own mind about Mrs. Schmaltz.

When Antoinette and her family moved to the big house, her mom partitioned a space on one side of their garage for a play house that seemed cozier, much superior to mine. It never occurred to me that Antoinette was envious of the play house my grandpa built.

I didn't remember that Antoinette couldn't have paper dolls. In my memory she had more of everything—more doll clothes, more furniture for her doll house, even a luxurious number of pens and pencils.

I do remember sitting on the cool linoleum floor in our dining room on stifling summer afternoons. Antoinette would stake out the space under the dining room table and sit cross-legged with her paper doll family. Her thick glasses would slip down and she'd push them up with her finger. My fly-away blonde hair hung in my face. The thick French braids wrapped in a crown on the top of her head kept her cool.

The black baby doll—we called them "rubber dolls" in those days—was my favorite in my doll family. She arrived with a name—Cassandra—an exotic name in that time and place. I have tried to trace her with no success. Toys and dolls were ordered from mail order catalogs. I assume Cassandra came from Sears Roebuck, compliments of Mom and Dad and Santa Claus.

I remember the sugar bread with embarrassment. A piece of Mom's homemade bread sprinkled with sugar and dribbled with a little water so the sugar would stick. That was my creation for times when there were no cookies, cake, or other sweets for snacks, nor soft butter to spread.

After Antoinette's initial response to my first letter, we resumed our childhood twin-minded imaginations without a pause for the intervening decades. Now we piqued each other's memories via email.

January 16, 2008
From: Antoinette
You asked when I left Balta . . . Two days after I graduated from high school! And I was so happy to be leaving home. My folks and I didn't see eye-to-eye about much of anything that last year. Mom was glad I was leaving, too. (I believe she was worried that I would marry a local boy.) She took me to Minneapolis/St Paul and stayed with me until I had a job and a place to live. That took all of a week. I got a job at Northwest Airlines and lived at the Catholic Guild for Young Women in St. Paul. I stayed at the Guild for about three months and when my work schedule changed, I moved into the upstairs of a private home within walking distance of work. I shared that with three girls from Wisconsin. It was through one of the girls that I met Duane later that fall. In late August, 1959, we were married. And, of course, Mom and Dad were not happy. Duane was a dairy farmer in Wisconsin . . .
P.S. Ask me questions about Nodak and I'll see what I can remember. I've dreamt about you several times in the last few weeks. So something must be trying to surface.

January 17, 2008
To: Antoinette
Thank you so much for the information. It is unimaginably good to be in contact with you . . . There is magic in it. I love hearing about your leaving Balta and going to Minneapolis. What courage! I am intrigued by our mothers. Let's explore that!

January 17, 2008
From: Antoinette
I'm sure I will disappoint you, as I'm not sure what I remember from my youth. I know Mom never liked living in Balta. In the early days whenever the women got together they spoke German, and, of course, Mom didn't, so she felt left out. I believe that your mom and Clara Hagel were about the only ones she coffeed with. As time went on she did make friends with others, and I don't think it was as bad as she imagined.

January 18, 2008
To: Antoinette
I do remember that Clara Hagel and your mom and mine coffeed. Clara was their mutual friend, but I always wished your mom and mine were best friends. I puzzle over that somewhat. They were both enlightened in ways many women were not. That German-Russian culture was stifling and isolated in so many ways. Your mom was a Protestant raised in Harvey; my mom had lived in several different small towns albeit in North Dakota, married to a Protestant. They were worldly by those standards. Harvey was only miles away. But it was a world away from Balta. And they read books! They both belonged to the Book of the Month Club.
I liked your mom. We didn't get a lot of compliments in those days. I wore pink for decades because your mom once told me I looked nice in pink!
You made pronouncements with your mom as the authority—things like, "My mom says I can wear lipstick in 7th grade (Coty orange/tangerine you would buy in Harvey)" or "My

mom said you can plan babies. Even Catholics. They can use the rhythm method . . ." That was definitely news to me, but I dared not reveal my ignorance nor the fact that my mom hadn't talked to me about that yet beyond giving me a little blue book to read. You had such confidence! Your mom was so knowing!

Do you remember the September of 6th grade when Sister Mary Dominic (the nuns ohhh scary women! I blame them for all my insecurities!) suggested that you and I be moved up to 7th grade? Your parents said no. Mine said yes. I even wondered about it at the time, because I thought your mom had good reasons for her decisions. That severed our friendship. I was pushed from playing dress-up to a grade with girls who were going to Rugby for accordion lessons and on the lookout for boys. Too young—then and later—fighting for position all through high school and college. Then we moved and I lost you . . . and here we are decades later.

January 18, 2008

From: Antoinette

Yes, I do remember when you got to skip a grade and I had to stay back. I was sooo hurt. The kids in the upper grades did not associate with the kids in the lower grades. And then you moved. More hurt.

. . . You puzzle over the fact that our moms weren't "best" friends, but I think they were too much alike to be "best" friends. When I think back on things my mother said, I think she was jealous of your mom. We will discuss this more at another time.

April 28, 2008

From: Antoinette

Hi!

. . . thinking about Balta . . . You asked if I thought it was a good place for kids to grow up. I guess . . . maybe that time was a good time to grow up. We could be outside and play all day with not much fear of terrible things happening to us.

Though I do remember when the Indians and Gypsies came to town we were kept inside so they couldn't "steal" us . . . as a teenager growing up there was a hassle as your folks knew what you had done even before you got home! And often the story was embellished to the point that you didn't recognize what you had done. And there was no point telling them that they had the story wrong because you did not question what they said! . . . And of course the opportunities weren't there for the young adults. For that reason I'm glad that I left right after high school graduation. But it was a good place to grow up.

Antoinette and I emailed all winter, stirring in our childhood and getting acquainted with our adult selves. In June 2008, on their annual motor-home trek from Virginia to North Dakota, Antoinette and her husband Duane spent several days with Monte and me. We had leisurely hours to find each other and for me to explore Antoinette's views about growing up in Balta. After that initial reunion, Antoinette and Duane parked their motor home in our driveway for a few days every summer.

In the meantime, I had been corresponding with Don Schaan. His life path has been rich with experience, from living in Europe both during and after his Army enlistment, to college and graduate school, then working as a social worker, community organizer for the Legal Aid Society, and advocate of Mental Patient Rights groups in the Los Angeles area. He found his work increasingly consisted of looking for funding rather than working with clients.

June, 2008
From: Don
Growing up on a farm, I wanted to have more of a one to one relationship with my income. I make something. I get paid for it. Like a farmer. I started finding unique tree branches, and lashing them together, then stringing leather between them and burning words and images into the leather. Later, I learned metal work. I became an artist . . . You can see some of the work I'm doing at: www.westernedgeart.com.

After learning to make a living with my hands, I couldn't see the point of going back into the professional world with all of its unstable funding, etc. And now I sublimate my social work needs by being quite active in my community and volunteering with activist organizations I agree with. We've been protesting this awful war (Iraq) since before it started . . .

While I interviewed my German-Russian family searching for *life stories,* Don delved into the history of his family and of Balta with an artist's eye. He called my attention to the metal grave markers in the Balta cemetery, referring to them as an early art form. The iron crosses, the *Eizenkreizen,* of the Germans from Russia are prevalent in the Dakotas especially in Catholic cemeteries. The early immigrants made the grave makers by heating and bending the metal which they held together with homemade clamps.

Don has discovered that although the cairn marking the Geographical Center of North America is in Rugby, the actual center is located at a large rock in a small lake six miles west of Balta. We did, indeed, grow up in the center.

While I have been obsessed with the Catholicism of our childhood, he has collected extensive information about the building itself, Our Lady of Mount Carmel Church. The original structure, built on the prairie four miles northwest of Balta in 1905, was deconsecrated and sold in auction to Don's grandfather, Walter Schaan, about 1920.

January 2013
From: Don
. . . It (the church) became our barn on the farm. While new siding recovered where the original "church" windows would have been, their unique outlines remained visible in the interior. It also retained a small, beautiful church window on the upper front of the "barn." My brother and I grew up with our sandbox being a frame of one of the large windows. Our sandbox was shaped like a boat . . . All these years, I have

looked for some photographs of the move of that church across the prairies to my Grandfather's farm. I haven't been able to come up with a photo . . . There was quite a neighborhood feud when they tried to move the altar from the old church to the new one at Balta. * It even turned violent when some tried to chop it up rather than allow it to be moved. There are repairs and signs of damage on the rear of the altar now in Balta.

Finding Antoinette was deliberate. Finding Don Schaan—serendipity or providence. As I reflected on my interest in Balta, in Antoinette, and in Our Lady of Mount Carmel Church, I remembered a comment Don Schaan made early in our correspondence.

August 16, 2008
From: Don
I feel a real affinity towards North Dakota and Balta, but I spent my entire young life there and still go back and have family and relatives there. I'm curious about the source and depth of your attachment to the area. You lived there for only a few short years. Maybe it even surprises you.

What *is* my attachment? Why the pilgrimage?

**In the year 1905 a church was built four miles north-west of the present Balta. The settlers gave the site or locality of their church the name: Selz . . . In 1919, the town of Balta having founded and the settlement in and around the town getting stronger and stronger, the old Selz church was given up. The new church in Balta was built and the parish at last was transferred to its present location in Balta. This transference did not come to pass without some friction and serious misunderstandings. However, in the course of time the whole congregation saw the wisdom of transference and everybody felt content.*
Historical Record of Our Lady of Mount Carmel Church, Balta, North Dakota
by Reverend Boniface Stuetz, April 27, 1938

4

GROWING UP CATHOLIC IN THE GEOGRAPHICAL CENTER

My childhood friend Antoinette has shattered my lifelong thesis. "Balta was a good place to grow up," she said. I wanted her to affirm my opinion that it was a dreadful place to grow up. An isolated community. An oppressive culture.

In finding her, I had envisioned a woman who shared my view, perhaps with humor and condescension. Now, forced to mine my memory for the positive place, I emailed Don Schaan and asked him to reflect on growing up in Balta.

> He responded:
> I graduated from high school in 1961. I knew I was a Hayseed and kind of out of place, or out of touch with the larger world. Remember, we didn't get electricity on the farm until around 1952, when I was almost 10 years old. We were one of the first in the community to have television, but that wasn't until 1959 or 1960. Part of the importance of that was just to watch American Bandstand, etc., just to see how others dressed and lived. I always knew I was going to go to college. (My dad was a college graduate.) But in 1961, I just knew I had to get out

of there for a while and experience the world. So I joined the army, "To See the World"—pre-Vietnam.

I left Balta *before* high school, excited and relieved, anxious to leave the small town and the nuns, especially the nuns, behind. Nuns are the main characters in the early scenes of my childhood recollections, and only two or three of them appear on the stage as gentle or kind. Their brand of discipline, blended with the potential punishment for disobedience here and the potential punishment for sin in the hereafter, fed my fears and anxiety. I was a nail-biting, bed-wetting kid with recurring nightmares—afraid of the dark, of heights, and of adult disapproval.

The Sisters of Mercy taught in the Balta public school for twenty years (1937-1957). They didn't proselytize to the handful of Protestant students, though their black veils and flowing black robes with the clinking rosary belts were powerful symbols. Discipline was paramount. The Catholic farm boys with their broken English annoyed them. The fidgeting town boys, sitting behind me and in front of me in desks bolted to the floor, got their hands smacked with a ruler regularly for a variety of infractions. I cringed when Eric Maier was called on to go to the black board. I just knew he didn't know the answer. Sister's scold filled the room with shame. I raised my hand for the next question.

Many of the farm kids came from homes where German was still the preferred language. I was embarrassed for them in the classroom and grateful I could read aloud without stumbling, avoiding Sister's scorn.

The only thing I envied the farm kids for was their winter bus ride—a horse-drawn covered wagon type thing on a sleigh with benches on each side of a small wood-burning stove—and their dinner buckets. I yearned to ride on that bus. No matter the weather, town kids had to walk home at noon for dinner, and in my story, the cold is always biting. Breath frozen white to scarf, glasses fogged, toes and nose tingling, I'd bang through the door and warm up in Mom's kitchen. Fried bread never tasted so good. I dreaded going back out into the cold and walking back to school for afternoon classes.

On Wednesdays after school, Catholic kids trudged to Our Lady of Mount Carmel where we had Catechism in the church basement. The coal-fed furnace couldn't compensate for the frigid temperatures. We huddled together on the pews in our coats and scarves during the endless winter. There we memorized the Ten Commandments, the Seven Sacraments, the Holy Days of Obligation, and the Baltimore Catechism—unrelenting rules. A powerful and punishing God. There we also heard the stories of saints and martyrs, the heroines young girls find in television and movies today.

The indoctrination in piety fed into my daydreaming. At the suggestion of a heroic life, especially one warranting fame and sainthood, my imagination took over. I could envision myself as Joan of Arc, "pious and grave beyond her years," the Sisters said, "divinely inspired, fearless and courageous." Or Saint Bernadette of Lourdes, the peasant girl who had visions of a beautiful lady in a rock declension, who turned out to be the Virgin Mary. Or, if I prayed enough to Our Lady of Fatima, maybe she would appear to me like she did to those three shepherd children in Portugal. She told the shepherd children to do penance and to make sacrifices to save sinners. The second time she appeared, she told them they must say the Rosary every day. The Rosary was the key to world peace.

Say the Rosary every day. That would be easy. I had spells of saying the Rosary every day—fleeting bouts of self-discipline to earn a place as a saint.

As for world peace. The nuns gave us a daily dose of the Cold War, the Korean War, and Stalin, the demon. I had a recurring nightmare—I am running, running, running to my aunt's house on a narrow gravel road with deep ditches filled with water on both sides of me. I can't swim. Giant, faceless, Communist men are chasing me. I wake up screaming just before I fall into the hole in Aunt Katie's outhouse.

My antennae were always out absorbing the atmosphere, eavesdropping on conversations, drawing disturbing conclusions.

I realized that my parents were misfits in Balta. Dad was a Mennonite in a Catholic town. Mom had lived in less insular places, albeit in small North Dakota communities.

My dad, an unassuming man of few words, would say later, "Those nine years in Balta were the unhappiest of my life." Mom blamed herself for those years. In the early 1940s, the gas station/service station where Dad worked in Alsen, North Dakota, closed. He made plans to go West with his brother. Jobs were plentiful for unskilled workers in the shipyards and housing industry in Seattle. Mom's parents begged her not to take their grandchildren away from them. She was young and afraid to leave. He had too little confidence and too much love to oppose her. Grandpa got him a job at the Farmers Union Oil Company. Mom convinced him to move to Balta.

Dad simply didn't fit in. Men hung around in the Farmers Union store speaking a blend of English and German. He didn't speak German. He found most of the men vulgar. Delivering gas to the farms in the area, he decided that many of them were cruel to their wives and "hard on their kids." And those men didn't respect him.

He was the kind of guy who stopped to watch the pheasants dance on the prairie or pick wild flowers to bring home to Mom. His work day began at dawn, delivering gas to the farmers. Then back to the Farmers Union to change tires and grease cars and do whatever car and truck fixing a man learned to do with no special education. "We never got ahead," he told me.

On Sunday nights, he listened to Reverend Charles Fuller and "The Old Fashioned Revival Hour." *Heavenly Sunlight/Heavenly Sunlight/Filling my soul with glory divine/Heavenly Sunlight/Heavenly Sunlight/Hallelujah Jesus is mine.*

One winter Saturday, Dad came home from Rugby with a table top RCA record player. He treated it lovingly, wiping the records gently with a special cloth before and after putting them on the turntable. I watched the arm come down and the needle touch the vinyl. I never touched the records or that handle, but the beat of John Phillip Sousa marches and Mario Lanza singing "The Student Prince" played in my head forever.

Books were Mom's gifts from infrequent and thus memorable trips to shop in Rugby. I still have *Heidi* by Johanna Spyri inscribed in her rounded, open-lettered, looped, easy-to-read script, *Niomi Annette Rohn 1946*. Mom read *Heidi, Heidi Grows Up,* and *Heidi's Children* to me over and over, and I inhabited the Alps before I could read about them myself. We didn't have a town library. We weren't allowed to take home the books on school shelves. The half-hour a day assigned to free reading in the class didn't satisfy the hunger of a story-loving child. Books were treasures.

I knew my mom was special because she belonged to the Book of the Month Club. She and Clara Hagel and Antoinette's mom, Eloie, waited impatiently for the next novel by Pearl S. Buck and Marjorie Kinnan Rawlings. They drank coffee and discussed the scandal over Betty Smith's *A Tree Grows in Brooklyn.*

Mom embraced people and life wherever she lived. She laughed easily and cried easily, too. "You can't be so thin-skinned, Betty," I can hear Dad say, comforting her for some slight, real or imagined.

She made a place for herself in Balta in spite of a spouse who didn't join the men at the local taverns, go to the Saturday night dances, or attend mass at Our Lady of Mount Carmel. She had been a 4-H club leader in Alsen, so she started a 4-H club and joined the Homemaker's Club. She and some of her women friends proposed that the town buy the site of a house that had burned down years before and create a park. Their husbands helped them clear the property of the burned foundation and the overgrown brush. Tall pines framed the area they flooded in winter for an ice rink.

On Saturday dance nights, Mom worked at Andy's Bar. She tried to help "make ends meet."

Mom is the only woman in a photo from the Rugby *Pierce County Republican* featuring the Balta School Board in the 1953 yearbook. She is seated next to Frank Schaan, president of the School Board and father of my email friend Don. Mom was the appointed treasurer. That appointment eventually proved the catalyst for Dad's escape from Balta.

Mom and Dad had happy times. I hear them now—the slap of the cards, playing canasta late into the winter nights with Joe and Clara Hagel. Mom's jolly laughter reaching my sister and me in our bunk beds in the bedroom of the small apartment. On Sunday nights before Christmas, when they were making fondant and dipping chocolates with Joe and Clara, I hovered in the background, fascinated and relishing their fun.

One January when the country roads had three-foot snow drifts and the temperatures were an unrelenting twenty degrees below zero, Mom's cousin, Vernice, and her husband Nick slept on the sofa bed in our living room for over a week. Vernice's fourth baby was due, and they didn't want to risk getting stranded on the farm without a doctor nearby.

Mom, Dad, Vernice, and Nick played canasta every night. I would lie at the foot of my top bunk as near to the open doorway as I could to listen to the conversation. Dad was always quiet, as was Vernice, but Nick and Mom sparred about everything. They disagreed about Joe McCarthy and his quest for Communists in the government, in colleges, and in the movie industry. Nick accused Mom of being soft on Communism. She argued that McCarthyism was a witch hunt.

"The threat's right here," he said.

"There's no Communist lurking in the backyard of every Protestant neighbor," she shot back, to the accompanying swish, swish of shuffling cards.

Interspersed with their voices raised in disagreement were the murmurs of "Your play," "I've melded," "Your discard." Mom's hearty laugh when the women were winning. Dad's chuckle when the men were ahead.

In my opinion, my mom was the smartest person in the world and right about everything. Nick was obviously narrow-minded. I didn't like him, and he didn't like me. "She's too big for her britches," he told Grandma. He regularly dismissed my eavesdropping presence with a smirk. "Nosy."

I also didn't like the demeaning way he treated my dad—cocky, know-it-all, authority-on-everything attitude. Once I overheard him mutter, "Well, you know who wears the pants in that family."

Vernice definitely didn't wear the pants. She wore an apron and rarely took it off. Farm life was hard work. She had six children in as many years, and Mom and Grandma "helped out" when they could.

In the early summer, we would go to the farm for the day "to do chickens." Mom, Grandma, and Vernice set up an assembly line. Axe in hand, Grandma chopped the heads off dozens of fowl that flopped all over the yard. Mom and Vernice grabbed them by the legs, dipped them in boiling water, pulled the feathers out, and removed the innards for canning or freezing.

Vernice's garden was even bigger than Mom's and Grandma's town plots. In the heat of August, they gathered on the farm to can tomatoes and corn. I can see them lifting their aprons to wipe the sweat off their foreheads, the steam billowing from the water boiling in the blue and white enamel canners on the stove. The curly rings of sticky, yellow flypaper dangled from the ceiling.

"Close that screen door. Quit running in and out. You're letting the flies in," they would yell at us kids.

Mom and Dad's "can't make ends meet" supper table discussions worried me. Even a hint of opportunity filled me with hope.

One time it was a Post Office job. Mom substituted for her friend Polly Roel in the Post Office when Polly needed a day off. When Polly decided to move from the area, I heard snatches of conversation. "Polly says this is perfect for me. Good salary. Vacation and sick leave. Even retirement benefits," Mom said, a lilt in her voice. "You have to take a Civil Service examination."

"That'll be a snap for you," Dad said.

She took the exam at the county seat in Rugby and waited for the results. I hurried home from school every day anxious for a hint of news.

She earned the highest score. The job was hers. Dad, always her humble champion, was so proud of her. Elation was fleeting. Then the bad news—George Mack had received added points to his score because he was a veteran. The job was his.

A couple years later, Uncle Walter was selling his prosperous used car business in Minot, North Dakota, and moving to Florida. Mom and Dad would be perfect proprietors. Dad knew cars from his years as a self-made mechanic. Mom was a whiz at bookkeeping. Minot! A city! Oh, the excitement, the possibility of living where we sometimes spent a summer Sunday picnicking in the park and listening to the city band.

Our only telephone hung on the wall in the Farmers Union store, so I don't know when the phone conversations were conducted. But I created and lived an imaginary city life for a few weeks at least—a real house, a school without nuns, band concerts every Sunday.

Children weren't privy to discussions, trivial or serious, but an attentive girl could know things. The kitchen, living room, and two bedrooms of our small apartment were separated by curtained doorways. I had my ears open and my antennae out for any sign of progress. Imagination and anticipation hovered over my daily routines. Day after day after day. Snippets of information. Uncle Walt. A bank loan. A down payment. Maybe Joe Gross would help out. Dad would ask him. Joe would. A trip to Rugby. The bank wouldn't give them the loan for the Minot business. I heard the noise of hope, then the quiet of disappointment. Life returned to normal.

The rhythm of life in Balta centered on Our Lady of Mount Carmel Church and the liturgical calendar. Our days and weeks were ordered by Saturday confession, Sunday Communion, weekly Catechism after school, and two weeks of Catechism in the summer. The God of the Ten Commandments dominated life and life was serious, fraught with the potential for sin. Black-garbed nuns with giant rosaries encircling their waists waited around every corner to catch you in venial sins which would send you to purgatory. Mortal sins and hell were just not fathomable.

But the Jesus celebrations, His birth, His death, and the honoring of His mother, gave us pageantry and procession, music and joyous excitement.

The four weeks of Advent were the longest month of the year. Pines weren't plentiful on the North Dakota prairie. Christmas trees were shipped in to the grocery store from a distant somewhere. "They weren't much," Dad would say. He often bought two trees. After the Farmers Union closed for the day, he would bring the trees inside, and I would watch him consider which tree to remodel. Then he would drill holes in the trunk of one, cut and insert branches from the other to create a perfectly shaped pine tree. He would drag his tree into the living room, put it in front of the window, and step back with a smile, admiring his work. Then he would unwind the string of lights, methodically attach each light to a branch, lights evenly spaced, while he reminisced about the Christmas trees of his boyhood. His parents decorated the tree. They opened the double doors into the living room on Christmas morning. The glory of that first sight, the tree lit with candles in the German Mennonite tradition, stayed with Dad forever.

For me, the 24th of December was the longest day of the year. "Find something to do . . . Go outside," Mom would say, annoyed and tired of my asking, "What time is it?"

Willing the hours to pass, I skated in circles, around and around and around, on the ice rink Dad had made behind the Farmers Union.

We had an early light supper in order to fast for Midnight Mass Communion. Then we walked to Grandma and Grandpa's house where Vernice, Nick, and their children joined us to open gifts. We received one or two things from Grandma and Grandpa; a doll, ice skates, or a game from Santa Claus, who came that evening; and something especially wonderful like a china story book doll—Snow White or Little Red Riding Hood—from Aunt Frannie. Her gifts came to us in mysterious packages all the way from Seattle.

After the gift opening we walked from Grandma and Grandpa's house to the church.

It's a crisp, cold night. Every footstep crunches. The snow sparkles under the street lights. My breath puffs out in clouds. The sky is filled with stars.

Grandpa opens the church door and the heat, the light, and the Christmas carols from the organ in the choir loft burst out to meet me. The church is packed—every pew full.

Instead of simply appearing from the sacristy at the altar, the altar boys process down the center aisle in their long, white, lace-trimmed surplices, carrying the United States and church flags, swinging the incense censor, followed by Father Boniface, his violet vestment of Advent replaced with white. We stand. We sing the traditional and familiar carols at the top of our lungs, because it is only on these special occasions the congregation sings. This is a night filled with music and singing.

Holy God we praise Thy name/Lord of all, we bow before Thee

Everyone from age six to eighty files out of their pews to receive Holy Communion. At the end of the mass, Father Boniface turns from the altar to face us. His booming voice leads the singing:

Oh, Holy Night/The Stars are brightly shining/It is the night of our dear Savior's birth.

We walk out into the snowy night. Back to Grandma and Grandpa's for a feast—cookies and fudge, *kuchen* and apple rolls, pickled herring, and homemade buns with summer sausage and cheese.

After Christmas—winter days of walking to school with scarves wrapped around our heads, only our eyes showing, breath freezing on scarves over our mouths, glasses fogging up. In our apartment, islands of warmth—right next to the oil burning space heater in the living room and next to the oven in the kitchen. Cold is a presence, like a person.

Finally, the early spring mud and thin ice on ditch water and Lent. Ash Wednesday. We go to mass before school and wear the ashes on our foreheads with superiority. The two Protestant boys in the class are excluded, though the nuns are careful not to talk about the significance of the day.

We don't eat meat on Wednesdays or Fridays during Lent, but that's no hardship for me. My favorite foods are Grandma's *kasnupla* (cheese buttons) and *nudla* (noodles) of all kinds, fried with potatoes, raised in a pan and eaten with raisin or prune sauce. Toasted cheese sandwiches and tomato soup make great lunches. Dad fries fish and picks the bones out for my sister and me. Canned salmon and tuna fish, creamed peas on toast, pancakes for supper, all of it works for me.

Every Wednesday night during Lent, we go to Our Lady of Mount Carmel to say the "Stations." Fourteen Stations of the Cross, plaques in bas relief, seven on each side wall of the church, retrace the steps of Jerusalem, depicting the death of Jesus: Jesus is condemned to death. Jesus takes up his cross. Jesus falls the first time. Jesus meets his sorrowful mother. Simon of Cyrene helps Jesus carry his cross. Veronica wipes the face of Jesus. Jesus falls the second time. The women of Jerusalem weep for him. Jesus falls the third time. Jesus is stripped of his clothes. Jesus is nailed to the cross. Jesus dies on the cross. Jesus is taken down from the cross. Jesus is placed in the tomb.

Two altar boys carry the kneeler and place it in the center aisle across from the Station. Father Boniface, in his violet vestment, kneels, makes the sign of the cross, folds his hands, and tells the story. His baritone, loud and clear, gives me goose bumps. And the story is in English. The Mass is in Latin. Sermons are in English and German. Ordinarily, during mass, I daydream and wander beyond the church, following the glint of sun through stained glass windows, into imaginary worlds. But I'm captivated by the mystery and immersed in the tragedy of this story of the crucifixion.

Father Boniface stands, the altar boys move the kneeler onto the next Station. Wednesday after Wednesday, the ceremony, each event, the murmur of the congregation's responses, *Our Father, who are in heaven/Hail Mary, full of grace/Glory be to the Father and the Son Who Art in heaven,* prepare me for the next dire event. By Good Friday, when He dies on that cross, I am living in the story.

I even attend morning Mass some days before school during Lent. Leaving the warmth of a flannel-covered feather comforter, when it is still dark and cold outside, contributes to my self-righteousness. Grandma is there sitting in a back pew, so I get immediate approval. She will see me walk in. I know she nods and smiles.

And in 5th and 6th grades, Antoinette and I are always waiting for the sign of a vocation. We are headed for the convent, if only we get the sign. Daily Mass during Lent just might put us in the realm of the martyrs or at least the children of Fatima.

We spend all of Holy Week in church, or so it seems to me—Holy Thursday, Good Friday, Holy Saturday. On Good Friday, the stores close from noon until 3 p.m., the hours Jesus died. We are encouraged to go to the church any time of the day to pray. Jesus on the cross is never alone. The church is always occupied, mostly by old women in black shawls murmuring the rosary. Jesus is dying. It's an eerie place. The statues are draped in black.

Mr. Sand doesn't ring the church bell, so even the town is silent. One church, one church bell. Sister Mary Anastasia doesn't play the organ, nor does the choir sing at mass on Holy Saturday. A wooden clapper, instead of a bell, signifies times to kneel or stand. It's chilly in the cavernous church. My daydreams are dark.

Easter morning the bell rings on and on. I walk to church with Mom, a skip in my step. I wear a hat, my new shoes from Sears Roebuck, and sometimes a new coat or one remodeled. Sister Mary Anastasia plays the organ with all stops open. Flowing white gauze drapes all the statues, and hundreds of candles light the front and side altars. I know I hear angels singing. Father Boniface and the altar boys have replaced the penitence and melancholy of violet vestments for joyful white.

In early May we begin practicing the songs for the May Crowning: *Oh Mary, we crown thee with blossoms today/Queen of the angels/Queen of the May.*

The grade school girls wear floor-length dresses with circlets of flowers instead of scarves on our heads. Grandma makes my dress. We carry baskets of flower petals to scatter in the path of the Queen of the May. Grandma makes my basket from an oatmeal box, cut down, and covered with crepe paper ruffles and chenille flowers.

The May Queen, a high school senior appointed by the nuns, wears a flowing, floor-length white dress. The high school girl attendants are attired in long pink and blue and yellow gowns like a spring bouquet. Except for the altar boys, this is the girls' day.

Our male classmates are relegated to their pews on the right side of the church where they join in our singing. The May Crowning songs are in English. By third grade, we all know them by heart. Everything is special about this day.

We line up in pairs behind Father Boniface in his white, lace-trimmed surplice, and the altar boys in white. We process down the aisle, singing, trying not to skip: *On this day oh Beautiful Mother/On this day we give thee our love.*

We worship the Blessed Mother with passion. She is serene. Beautiful. Gentle. Sitting at the edge of heaven, loving us so much, she is willing to give us a hand up.

Women clutch their rosaries, say Hail Marys like a mantra. Pray to her for comfort and help. Our God is all powerful, but He is removed from women's cares. His mother is approachable—a woman, a mother, one of us.

At the end of May, we tear out of the school doors. Oh, glorious summer. Then, except for the depot agent's boys and a couple Protestant farm kids, we sober ourselves for two long weeks of Catechism, restless for freedom.

We sit in rows of desks in the school room. We begin and end the day with the Sign of the Cross, the Lord's Prayer, and a Hail Mary. Sisters Mary Dominic and Anastasia in their formidable black habits and veils, rosary belts clicking as they walk up and down the aisles between desks, drill us on the Ten Commandments and the Seven Sacraments and the Holy Days of Obligation.

They call on us to answer questions, or we bravely raise our hands. The warm summer breeze wafts in the open windows. No whispering. No fidgeting. I try desperately to pay attention and not daydream myself out of there. The quiet is broken by the meadow larks singing summer.

We get our first copy of the *Baltimore Catechism* the summer between first and second grades, when we can finally read. We memorize. Fifty years later, any kid brought up Catholic can recite the opening pages. *Who made us? Who is God? Why did God make us? What must we do to gain the happiness of heaven?*

That summer of 1947, Grandma Bertsch sewed my First Communion dress and veil. She made a pattern from newspaper and cut it from Mom's wedding dress. I had to stand still in her sewing room for hours (or so it seemed to a seven-year-old), whining while she pricked my bare legs with pins to check the hem of the dress. In a miniscule black and white photo in an old album, I am standing on the church steps in white anklets and white shoes, wearing that homemade dress. A circlet of flowers holds the veil which falls to the hem just above my knees.

We practiced for First Communion the entire two weeks of Catechism that summer, but it wasn't just about Communion. It was about another big "C," Confession. We walked in twos behind Sister Mary Ellen down the street from the school to the church. There we sat in the back pew, waiting our turn to confess our sins to Father Boniface. The confessional was like a phone booth with three sections. Sister sat in the middle section where Father would sit on the "for real" day. A confessor knelt on a bench on each side. Inside was shadowy dark. You could hear the murmur of the person on the other side, see the shadowy outline of Father Boniface when he slid the little door open to hear your confession. And you waited —breathless, heart banging.

He would say, "Bless you, my child."

You had to answer, "Bless me, Father, for I have sinned. This is my first confession." And then tell him your sins which you had pondered while sitting in the back row, waiting your turn.

He would listen and assign a penance, like three Hail Marys. Then he would say, "Go in Peace." You were to open the door, go back to your pew with your head bowed, say the penance prayers, stand up to go home, genuflect beside the pew, make the sign of the cross at the holy water fountain before you went out the door. So many things to remember.

We practiced Communion too. We marched down the center church aisle behind Sister Mary Ellen, sitting in again for Father Boniface, and the altar boys.

"Look straight ahead. Fold your hands. When it's your turn, lift your head and close your eyes. Open your mouth," Sister said. "Father Boniface will put the wafer on your tongue. You must not touch it with your teeth. You must not chew it. It will soften. Swallow it. Bow your head. Wait at the Communion rail until the entire class has received Communion. Stand up together. Do not look around. Walk back to your pew with your hands folded and your head bowed. Enter from the back aisle in the same order you came in."

What if I did something wrong? What if my teeth touched the wafer? What if I choked? What if I wet my pants? (I had worried about that ever since I felt the warm, wet humiliation running down my white stockings on a Memorial Day procession from the church to the graveyard.)

All that practice. All those rules. All that anticipation. Saturday night Confession. No food or water until Sunday morning. Don't forget and drink water. A beautiful new dress with a veil like a bride. I would only wear that dress one time.

Later that summer I spent a week at Bible School with my Mennonite cousins in Alsen. We sat in little chairs around a table. Like Catechism, Bible School started with prayer. Pretty young Lydia Schmeiss made up a prayer, talked to Jesus. And we memorized Bible verses like Dad's favorite:

John 3:16 For God so loved the world, that He gave his only begotten Son, that whosoever believeth in him should not perish but have everlasting life.

And we sang: *Zaccheus was a wee little man/a wee little man was he/He climbed up in the sycamore tree to see/what he could see/And when the Lord came passing by . . .*

Mrs. Schmeiss passed out construction paper, colors, and scissors. We made a sycamore tree for Zaccheus to climb.

Mrs. Schmeiss talked about accepting Jesus Christ as your personal savior. I loved Lydia Schmeiss. I wanted her to love me. On the last day, when she asked if anyone would like to come forward to profess their faith and accept Jesus as their personal savior, I stood up. I'd resisted the gesture all week. Three of us walked solemnly to the front of the room and knelt to pray. We bowed our heads. Mrs. Schmeiss prayed over us, and we walked back to our seats around the table.

The first Sunday at home in Balta after vacation with my Mennonite family, I walked down the street to Our Lady of Mount Carmel with Grandma Bertsch. I skipped. Slowed down to walk beside her. She took my hand.

"*Mon lieb,*" she said, "so good you can go to Communion with me now." And it was. And I knew that it wouldn't be a good idea to tell her that I had spent the past week in Bible School and that I had accepted Jesus Christ as my personal savior.

As a child, I didn't suffer qualms or guilt, ironic as that is considering that I claimed my Catholic education had instilled guilt like concrete. Alsen and Balta were different worlds. No one told me how to conduct myself, nor warned me of consequences. I wanted the love and approval of both families. I enjoyed the limelight wherever it happened to fall on me, and I was self-protective. Perhaps those were the seeds of my religious ambivalence.

I loved to walk into Our Lady of Mount Carmel Church with its stained glass windows and the familiar life-sized Jesus on the cross and the Blessed Mother on the side altar.

Grandma Bertsch put on a dark dress for Mass and stood in front of the mirror attached to her dresser to put long, black-beaded pins in her black hat with the hint of a veil to hold it on her head. Women covered their heads for mass. The old women wore black babushkas. Grandma and Mom wore hats on Sundays, scarves tied under the chin for daily Mass.

Grandma Bertsch stopped just inside the door of Our Lady of Mount Carmel, dipped her hand into the fountain of holy water, made the sign of the cross, and then, hands folded, proceeded down the aisle where she genuflected before she entered one of the back pews. The silence in the church was broken only by coughs and throat clearings.

Before I started school and sat in the front pews with the other kids, Grandma let me stand on the kneeler beside her to see the altar. White-robed Father Boniface sat on a bench with the altar boys. When the bell rang, he stood at the altar, faced the crucifix, hands folded high, his back to us, and began the prayers of the Latin mass. Grandma followed in her missal. Latin responses hummed in monotone around me. Old women in black dresses and shawls surrounded me, comforting and safe, but I wrinkled my nose with the musty whiffs of ancient wool. Only the choir sang—in Latin—from a choir loft above us.

I liked the small white Swiss Mennonite church in Alsen, North Dakota too. Grandma and Grandpa Rohn, dad's parents, lived there, a small village 150 miles east and north of the Geographical Center. The Swiss Mennonite Church, with a modest steeple and a bell, was one of two churches, the other, Lutheran. Inside, a simple black cross hung at the front between the tall, narrow windows reaching to the ceiling. Center pews, two side aisles with pews on each side. An intimate size. A small nave where the minister sat on one of two chairs to the side of a lectern. A wall board front right with titles of the morning songs and page numbers posted for everyone to read, a piano on the left.

Grandma Rohn came down the stairs in her navy blue church dress, her long white hair pulled into a knot at the back of her head, secured with a comb on each side. By that time of the morning, Grandpa was ensconced in his brown leather chair in the living room, papers and magazines on a table at his side, his crutches leaning against the arm. I had never known him without his crutches. He had fallen from a grain elevator before I was born.

I don't recall words between them beyond information like, "Dinner's ready." And when it was just the three of us, Grandpa ate his three meals at the dining room table. Grandma and I ate in the kitchen.

It was a silent house, though Grandma whistled. I could hear her when I woke in the upstairs bedroom, and I knew the oatmeal would be in the blue and white speckled pan pushed to the back of the cook stove to keep warm. She didn't chatter. She rarely carried on conversation with me. She wasn't a talkative, touching kind of Grandma, but during one of my summer visits when I awoke each morning with pink eye, she sat by the bed with a white enamel pan and gently washed away the encrusted pus with a flannel cloth and warm water. This meager evidence of love was apparently sufficient for me.

We walked to church side-by-side. I sat next to her in the church pew intrigued by the commotion of people turning to greet each other with quiet nods and murmured hellos. When the pianist struck the first chords on the piano, the minister stood and faced the congregation with arms open, inviting us to stand and sing.

When the trumpet of the Lord shall sound/and time shall be no more/
When the morning breaks eternal bright and fair/
When his chosen ones shall gather over on the other shore/
When the roll is called up yonder I'll be there.

Two churches in two small towns on the North Dakota prairie, both settled by Germans from Russia. The child of the uncommon marriage of Catholic and Mennonite, I moved and maneuvered in both churches and families, like a chameleon.

In our Catholic hometown, my sister and I lived three blocks from Grandma and Grandpa Bertsch. We ran in and out of their house daily. Their kitchen table yielded luscious food and attention, card games and checkers, Grandpa's jokes and cartoon drawings, sometimes help with homework. On Sundays and holidays, Vernice, Nick, and their children joined us.

Sometimes on holidays we went to Alsen. At Grandma and Grandpa Rohn's, many aunts and uncles and cousins filled the house. Kids were not "to get underfoot," but if you were quiet, you could hover in the doorway of the living room or even sit quietly on the floor next to your dad, a haze of cigarette smoke and Grandpa's pipe mingling with the talk about the Korean War or the state of the crops.

In the kitchen and dining room, Grandma Rohn and the aunts stirred pots on the stove, buzzed in and out of the pantry, put stacks of plates and silverware on the table, talking as they worked. The kitchen conversation was more interesting than the living room—family gossip, small town news—a young farmer in a car accident, hit head-on, his pregnant wife killed. The baby died too. A boy down the road ran away because he didn't want to be drafted. About that time, an aunt would notice your interest and command, "Find something to do." The "something" was Rook, dominos, or Chinese checkers. My Mennonite family didn't believe in playing cards because of some strange connection to gambling, but Rook was acceptable.

When our boy cousins were tired of us, my sister and I sat on the dining room floor with a needle and thread, sorting and stringing necklaces from Grandma's button box.

When the aunts announced dinner, Grandpa and the uncles got up from their chairs and moved to the big dining room table for the first shift. Aunts trooped in from the kitchen with hot mashed potatoes and gravy and creamed corn. They ate with the kids at the second shift.

The Christmas my cousin Howard came home on leave from the Navy, I stood in the doorway most of the first setting just to look at him. He was so handsome in his white uniform with the blue stripes on the big collar, a man now, sitting at the table with Grandpa and the uncles.

Uncle Laverne always said the grace, a personal kind of communication thanking Jesus for Howard's safe return home, for the family, the food. When he got to the forgiveness for our sins part, we knew the prayer was almost over. Uncle Laverne, I thought, had a special relationship with Jesus.

We prayed before meals at my Catholic family's table, too—the same prayer every meal. We made the Sign of the Cross and prayed together, the same prayer my friend Antoinette and her family said at their house.

Prayer was essential in both families. I didn't make the Sign of the Cross when I was with my Mennonite family. No one told me not to—I just knew. I wasn't troubled by the differences—a friend-like Jesus in one place, a father-like God in the other. A formal relationship with God. Spontaneous prayer to Jesus. I had it all.

Religion, church, nuns, all played a role in ending our years in Balta. Once a month, on Friday afternoon, we had movies in school: *Heidi, The Courage of Lassie, Easter Parade.* The movie theatre in Rugby was sixteen miles away, a long distance on gravel roads, and few kids went to movies.

One week, the Sisters asked us each to bring twenty cents for the movie. I heard Mom tell my dad, "The School Board has already paid for those films. I wrote the check myself."

It "stuck in her craw," she would say if she talked about it in later years, though she preferred to forget about it. The Catholic guilt and embarrassment about the commotion she caused made her want to forget it ever happened.

At the time though, she couldn't "let it go."

"The more I think about it, the madder it makes me," she said. But challenging a nun was unthinkable. They were in charge and always right. But this wasn't right. Mom had to do something. It was a public school. The School Board had to be in charge of the public school.

On Monday afternoon before the Sisters said the Angelus in their chapel, she walked to their house, rang the bell and asked for Sister Mary Dominic, the school principal. Mom rarely exchanged more than a few words with the nuns. You sent your kids to school and to Catechism and never interfered or questioned their authority.

It took the passion of her anger for this confrontation. She sat in the sun porch and waited for Sister to sweep through the door in her black veil and flowing gown.

"Mrs. Rohn, what can I do for you?"

"I understand the kids have been asked to bring money to pay for the Friday movies. The School Board has already paid for those films," Mom blurted out in a rush, before she lost her courage. "You shouldn't be charging the kids. Some of them will have a hard time coming up with twenty cents. Some families have six and seven kids in school."

Sister Mary Dominic remained standing. She flicked the black veil from her face with the tip of her hand. "There are expenses involved, Mrs. Rohn. The Sisters are making cookies and there will be pop."

Sister Mary Dominic, confident, in charge, the final authority, didn't flinch, standing there, looking down at Mom perched at the edge of the porch chair.

Mom didn't wait to be dismissed. "I have to report it to the School Board." She stood up, turned away, walked out the door and down the street to Clara Hagel's house where she burst into tears.

"You went to Sister Dominic about those movies? Why did you do that? There'll be hell to pay. No telling what they'll do." After that first reaction, Clara relaxed. "It'll be all right," she sympathized, glad it wasn't her in this mess and not sure she wanted to be a public ally.

By the time I got home, I could tell Mom had been crying. A scary thing. I didn't dare ask. I wasn't supposed to know anything.

The next day Father Boniface came by the Farmers Union, and Dad brought him back to our apartment. That was like having the pope visit. Dad wasn't one of the priest's card-playing friends. As far as I knew, Father Boniface never went to anyone's house. He patted me on the head when he came in the door. Dad led him through the kitchen to the living room. He heaved his heavy bulk into the only easy chair. Mom sat on the sofa. Dad stood by the door.

Dad nodded his head at me. I didn't have to be told to leave the room. Dread walked with me, but I listened from around the corner near the doorway. Father Boniface's booming voice carried.

"You know how these nuns are, Lizbet. Don't make trouble. Let it go, Lizbet," he said. "Let it go."

After that Mom even went to Eloie Schmaltz, though they had never been close friends. Eloie was a convert. Maybe she would be sympathetic. Mom must have been desperate for allies, I thought. "Even Eloie says I should let it go," Mom said. "Even Ma (my grandma) is disgusted with me for creating such a stir." No allies. A solid front for the hierarchy of the church.

Mom was obsessed with leaving Balta after that. She went on a quest to find Dad a job somewhere, anywhere. They searched the want ads of the *Grand Forks Herald.*

Hope infected me too. I ached for us to move. The town whispers about my mother made me self-conscious and the kid-glove treatment the nuns gave me was worse. Most of all though, I was infused with excitement about the possibilities—a new and different place, bigger and interesting. Maybe we could live in a real house instead of an apartment.

They found the job in a town in the Red River Valley, only 150 miles from Balta. Dad never elaborated on the sequence of events, but he would say with a *harrumph* that he owed a lot to the nuns because they pushed Mom and him into changing their lives. "I never liked it there," he said.

5

TRUTH AND FICTION

Once you begin to write the true story of your life in a form that anyone would possibly want to read, you start to make compromises with the truth.

Ben Yagoda

The poetry, fiction, and nonfiction pieces in the following pages have been previously published.

Grandma's Apron

Grandma's apron
is soft as brushed silk now
faded beyond recognition
of flour sacks she used
for her aprons and my dresses
patterned from Sears Roebuck
chosen from glossy wish book pages

the apron covered her
from shoulder to hem
wrapped around her considerable girth
solid, stable, dependable
standing at the kitchen table
patting *kuchen* into pans
deftly forming rolls with strong hands

she tied the apron
around her like armor
went directly to the kitchen
to serve the lunch the day
her daughter, my mother was buried

the apron appeared in my kitchen
when she no longer had one of her own
ready to supervise holiday dinner
she would slip into the room at dawn
where I was indulging in self-pity

I asked how women coped in her day
we had children to feed
meals to prepare work to be done
you do what you have to do
you put on your apron and get to work

Published by *The Talking Stick,* 2008

Marriage

circa *1937-1987*

When she was seventeen
she fell in love
with his *difference.*

He was a foreigner in a place where
crude men cared more
about barns than houses
drank beer and vodka in Andy's Bar
after confession on Saturday night
their women waiting in cars on Main Street
after they sold the eggs and cream.

He was born again
didn't go to confession
or drink liquor
delivered gas to the farmers
stopping in the fields
on his way home
to pick wildflowers.

She tired of flowers and softness
yearned for strength
wished he'd *wear the pants in the family*
now and then.

But at the end
he cleansed the wound carefully
washed gently where her breast had been
and kissed her goodnight with a prayer.

Published by *Dust & Fire,* 2010

The Day the Nuns Wore Dresses

Bergdorf, North Dakota
1948

"Communists behind it," Johanna's dad said, scooping nails into a bag. "They're against religion. This anti-garb thing is just the beginning. They want to run the nuns out of our schools."

My best friend Johanna lived in an apartment above her dad's hardware store on Main Street. We were bored with the hot summer afternoon, and we were crouching in the stairway eavesdropping on the conversations below.

Lately, it seemed like everybody was talking about Communists. Like the depot agent might be one and John Placek, who lived on the farm just outside of town and didn't go to mass at St. Mike's, might be one. I finally worked up the courage to ask Mom about that St. Mike's thing since Daddy didn't go to mass either.

"Ignorance," she said. "Around here, if you aren't German and Catholic, you must be a Communist . . . and you don't have to repeat that!"

But what about this garb thing and the nuns? They were about the most important people in town, or at least at school and church, and that was the sum of a kid's life.

When the nuns swept down the street in their flowing black robes to buy groceries or pick up their mail, even the grownups stepped aside and muttered, "Good morning, Sister" or "Good afternoon, Sister."

When they came by Johanna's hardware store, we'd interrupt our hopscotch or push our wagons off the sidewalk to make way. If Johanna's dad was outside, they greeted him by his first name.

My dad didn't know the Sisters by name. In fact, my dad and the depot agent were the only Protestants in town. Maybe six farm kids in our school were Protestants. Grandma said the Protestants were the reason the

Sisters might not be allowed to wear their habits anymore. That's what the anti-garb law meant. Mom and Grandma argued about it all summer.

"It's a public school," Mom said. "Some people don't want nuns teaching at all."

"Do they think the 'Catholic' will rub off on their kids if the nuns wear their habits? I suppose you are going to vote for it," Grandma said.

"It might seem ridiculous to you, Ma, but enough people petitioned to get it on a ballot, so we'd better take it seriously. We're just lucky they can teach here at all. I don't think there's another place in the country where nuns teach in public schools. This vote's making national news. Eloie Schmaltz has a cousin in Chicago, and she says the *Chicago Tribune* has been covering it all summer. They're saying the vote is dividing the State—Protestants against Catholics."

Mom argued with Uncle Nick about it too. He said he was "furious," that the government thought they could tell the nuns how to dress.

"There's a teacher shortage. They're better educated than most of the teachers around here. We should be glad they're willing to teach in this small town."

Mom came back with her public school speech and they ended that conversation with words I'd heard from him before, "Women shouldn't mess in politics."

The day of the vote was like a holiday only we didn't have to go to church. Every parking place was filled on Main Street. Kids ran all over while their parents stood in line to vote in the town hall.

People were standing around in Hager's grocery and the Farmers Union and Johanna's hardware store and Johnny Schaan's Standard Oil on the corner. Nobody paid attention to us kids. We ran from one place to the other, reconnecting with farm friends we hadn't seen since the end of school.

Mom said she didn't even want to talk to Grandma the next day if the vote passed. It did—"with big margins," Daddy said. "There are only seventy-five nuns teaching in the state, but they can't wear their habits to school anymore."

All summer we heard the adults talking about the Sisters having to wear real people clothes, but they looked the same at mass on Sundays, sitting in the tenth row on the girls' side of the church.

We were hyper with curiosity and excitement on Monday morning, the first day of school. The fifth grade teacher was always Sister Mary Anastasia—old, wrinkled Sister Anastasia who especially hated boys and held a ready ruler to slap hands not working and tap heads not minding their own business. She had the kind of reputation that kept a kid awake half the night before the first day of school and made the oatmeal churn in your stomach at breakfast.

We were whispering and restless before the bell rang, waiting for Sister Mary Anastasia, but when the door opened into the fourth and fifth grade classroom, we were stunned into silence. The only sound was the meadow lark singing in the field outside when the stranger walked in. We didn't dare look at each other.

She had tight curled gray hair, like she'd taken the metal curlers out and not combed. It took us a few minutes to figure it out. A wig! We'd never seen anyone wear a wig except for a costume party.

She seemed fatter and shorter than the Sister Mary Anastasia we knew too. The black skirt and white blouse didn't disguise her shape like the robes of the black habit. Her lips were tight, and she had an even crabbier face than usual, just daring us to snicker. As if we would. We'd be struck dead for sure. But without the swishing black robe and the big rosary hanging from the belt, and with that strange hair, she wasn't as scary as she'd been before. My stomach uncurled.

That first day we made a game of trying to get a look at all five nuns. What color hair do you think Sister Mary Ellen will have? What kind of dress will the principal, Sister Mary Dominic, wear?

Fifth graders weren't allowed in the basement sixth to eighth grade classrooms, or on the second floor high school. We had to make excuses to go to the outhouse hoping to get a glimpse or linger in the hallway on our way home for lunch.

Johanna and I peeked into the first and second grade room. Our favorite teacher, Sister Mary Ellen, had emerged like a butterfly from the stiff white face shell and black robe. We looked at each other with delight. Young and pretty. Like June Allyson. We would adore her.

Sister Mary Dominic tromped the halls as usual between her classes, making sure order was maintained, silence absolute, and no one loitered in the hallways on their way to the outhouses behind the school. She looked so strange with her head freed from the white band beneath the black veil and the bib under the chin. Her gray and black hair was pulled back in a bun thing, with her neck showing. We'd never seen her neck. And her blouse—there were gaps between the buttons. Breasts? Nuns have breasts?

She was even bigger in real clothes than in her habit, but I could feel a difference. She was still like a sentinel at the head of the stairs, but without her armor, daring us to show we noticed the change.

Johanna and I couldn't wait to get out of school to talk about the day. The mysterious life of nuns had always provided endless topics of interest, but this was new ground. Do you think they look in mirrors now? What do they wear in bed? How long is the hair underneath the wigs? Do you think they still shave their heads? How do the wigs stay on if their heads are shaved?

But they only needed wigs that first year. On the first day of sixth grade, we could see that the Sisters all had their own hair. Johanna and I exchanged furtive grins when Sister Mary Agatha pushed her soft brown curls back from her face and repeatedly ran her fingers through her hair.

Vanity? A vain nun? Huh, not a saint. Just a woman after all. Life was more confusing every year. Maybe all Protestants weren't Communists either.

(This short story, published by *The Talking Stick* in 2007, is based on fact. On July 2, 1948, an Anti-Garb Law passed in the state of North Dakota. A headline in the *Chicago Tribune* read "North Dakota Vote OKs Ban on Nun's Garb in Public Schools." *The New York Times* read "North Dakota Nuns to Adopt Civilian Dress in Order to Teach Under New State Curb.")

The Light in the Farmyard: A Winter Memory

I recall Dad reminiscing about that winter of 1950 when I was ten. Record snowfall, he said, with six-foot high banks in some places. The National Guard came in to help open the roads in rural North Dakota.

My own recollection is of a winter trip, my five-year-old sister and I hopping impatiently around the car, snow crunching under our feet, while Daddy puts suitcases in the trunk. We're going to Grandma and Grandpa's in Alsen for Christmas.

All of our cousins will be there. We'll play Rook and Sorry. Eat the popcorn balls and divinity Grandma only makes at Christmas. Spend Christmas afternoon checking on the uncles who are cranking the ice cream freezer on the back porch, then clambering in the kitchen for our first tastes from the dasher, and carrying our full, white soup bowls to the dining room table.

It's a bright, clear, snow-squeaking day, and the heater in the old Hudson isn't very effective, so we wear our snow pants, boots, and coats in the car. Daddy bundles us in blankets in the back seat. We hold our breath, afraid the sputtering motor won't catch. Sometimes it doesn't. Sometimes winter trips have to be cancelled.

Daddy never curses, just patiently works his magic with motors, and the Hudson doesn't let us down. Though faltering and chugging, it takes off.

The snow banks on the sides of the two-lane road are higher than the car. We are cocooned in a white tunnel.

Mama and Daddy sing. They always sing in the car, their harmony lulling us into half sleep, deepest content.

"On a hill far away stood an old rugged cross . . ."

"One day at a time, sweet Jesus . . ."

"When the trumpet of the Lord shall sound . . ."

Gospel. The irony of their choice in music won't occur to me until many years later.

Mama is a Catholic, and Catholics don't sing gospel in 1950. Dad is Mennonite. Theirs is a "mixed marriage." I am certainly aware of that. Catholic Grandma Bertsch told me that Lutherans have bedbugs. I once overheard my Mennonite grandma and the aunts discussing the disgusting practice of Catholics kneeling to worship statues.

Our home in a prairie village is a community of German-Russian Catholics. But Daddy doesn't go to mass with us, and as far as I can figure out, the depot agent and my dad are the only people in town who don't go to mass.

On Sunday mornings, I wish he were with us, sitting on the men's side of Our Lady of Mount Carmel Church with the other dads, but Sunday nights are fun. Sometimes he makes popcorn and orange pop floats and then reads us stories from a big and beautiful Bible storybook with colored photos of Samson and Delilah and David and Goliath. And Mama crochets while we listen to Charles E. Fuller's "Old Fashioned Revival Hour" on the radio in the living room.

It's unlikely the strains of "Heavenly sunlight, heavenly sunlight filling my soul with glory divine" are filling any other living room in town. Our family is different.

My dad is different from the other men I know. He doesn't go to the tavern after work or hang out there on Saturday nights when the farmers come to town. He and Mama don't go to the dances at the tavern where my friends' parents go, and he doesn't call her "Ma" or "the old lady" either.

Once at Grandma B's when I was lying on the floor of the bedroom with my ear to the heat register listening to the conversation in the living room below, I heard my Uncle Nick talking about Dad. "Well, he sure doesn't wear the pants in the family," he said with a laugh.

Later, working up my courage, I speculate about the matter of men wearing the pants and what that means to Mama. She responds sarcastically with "Yes, German men wear the pants. They're the boss. And a pregnant woman can sit at the table with a child on her lap and one in a high chair beside her and no man will lift a finger to help." Even a ten-year-old knows what constitutes a "touchy subject."

But right now, we are in the car, just the four of us. And there are cousins and aunts and uncles waiting. A warm house full of noise and commotion and Grandma's pantry with jars of big round sugar cookies, molasses cookies, and *pfeffernusse.*

Even in the summer, the trip from our house to the cousins is long, one hundred miles across the prairie on narrow two-lane gravel roads. Today the snow is blowing.

Half awake, I suddenly realize that Mama and Daddy aren't singing, and I hear the wind. Excitable, talkative Mama is silent. Daddy is gripping the steering wheel, and the car is bumping from side to side. It is so quiet, and I can also see my breath. Pretending to smoke though, as we often do in the winter cold, doesn't feel like the thing to do.

The windows are frosted up, so I scratch a peephole with my fingernails. Daddy is scraping the front windshield. That heavy old Hudson jumps one way, then another, hits a bank of snow, and stops, nearly throwing us off the seat.

Mama and Daddy are talking now, quietly. I strain to hear what they are saying. "We're stuck. I can't get us out," Daddy says.

"What are we going to do?"

"I used to deliver gas near here," Daddy says. "There's a farm about a mile down the road, I think."

"But it's getting dark."

"We can't stay in the cold car."

"But the snow will be over the kids' boots. Vickie's too small to walk that far."

"I'll carry her."

Daddy opens the back doors for us, and they wrap our long woolen scarves around and around our heads so only our eyes are uncovered.

Daddy picks my sister up. Mama takes my hand. We set out with Daddy leading the way.

"Stay right behind me," he says. "There's a yard light ahead. I can see it. Betty, are you okay?"

I wonder fleetingly about his concern, but nothing seems amiss to me. She is wearing her usual nylon stockings, rubber boots like ours over her shoes, a pretty scarf on her head, and her new leather Christmas gloves.

"I see the light."

"I know there's a farm."

"We'll be there in no time."

"Are you okay? Hold onto the back of my coat."

I can't see anything but Mama now right in front of me in the swirling world of white. We can't talk. I just hold onto her coat. The snow is over my knees. I lift my feet high and concentrate on staying in the track Mama and Daddy are making. Take big steps. Breathing is hard work. But I'm not frightened. Daddy said there is a farm ahead, and that's where we are going.

And then—there is a building—right in front of our faces. Daddy pounds on the door. A large man opens the door and pulls us inside. Daddy peels off our coats, boots, and mittens, touches our faces, and feels our hands and feet. Someone opens an oven door of a big, shiny chrome and black kitchen stove, wraps my sister and me in blankets, and sets us on chairs in front of it.

Daddy is hugging Mama and rubbing her hands. "Let me look at your legs, Betty." She is crying. I've never seen her cry and that is fleetingly upsetting, but the big kitchen is full of people—men, women, kids. Too many to count. No way to figure out if they all live here. And the light in the kitchen is shadowy, the oven hot, and I'm sleepy.

Women bustle around putting food in kettles on the stove, getting dishes out of cupboards. They move kerosene lamps to the table. Someone puts two Sears Roebuck catalogs on a chair for my sister to sit on, and we sit between Mama and Daddy. Food is served, but I am never hungry in strange houses. A woman pours milk into our glasses from a big jar. I don't say a word, but Daddy knows my mind, leans over, and whispers, "It's okay. These are good people. It's clean milk from their own cows."

Someone suggests we bow our heads and hold hands. They pray. Daddy thanks the Lord for our safety, for the welcome of the farmer and his family, for the food we are about to receive.

The talking around the kitchen table is a quiet buzz in the warmth and the lamplight.

"We got stuck about three miles from here," one man says. "We're lucky the farm is so close to the road."

"We were just behind you and so glad it was still daylight," another man says. "What time did you lose power?"

Did Dad see a yard light? I'll never know. I do know I wasn't frightened or traumatized by the experience. Apparently, I had trust and faith in Dad's ability to take care of us (no matter the perception of others that he didn't wear the pants in the family). Nor was I traumatized by the extremes in our lives, although that fascinates me today—two immigrant families separated in place and in fact by strong religious and cultural differences.

Reflecting on that winter storm, I begin to understand the kind of man my dad was and why my strong-minded and rebellious mother married him against the objections of his family and hers. It was an uneasy union, but perhaps protected by love of music and the harmony they could create. Gospel still comforts me.

Memoir published in
Winter: A Season of Writing on the Prairie
by Lake Region Writers' Group
Devils Lake, North Dakota, 2005

Dancing in the Dark

Balta, North Dakota, 1951

"We need the money, Harold. You know there aren't any jobs around here after potato picking's over." I hear Mama say that to Daddy. She quits talking when I walk into the room. Not like Grandma. Grandma just switches to German if she doesn't want me to know what she's talking about.

Mama and Daddy don't speak German in our house. They don't want me to learn it either. There was a big war, and Germans were enemies. No sense calling attention to yourself, Mama says. We're Americans and Mama and Daddy see no reason for a kid in our family to learn German. In school the farm kids talk German at recess, but they get in big trouble if the Sisters hear.

"I'm going to work at Andy's Bar on Saturday nights for the dances," Mama finally tells me days later. I ask her what she's going to do there. "Just serve drinks from about 9 o'clock to 1 o'clock. You'll be asleep. You won't even know I'm gone." I will know she's gone. And I won't like it.

After Confession, the men hang out at Andy's Bar while the women go to Schaan's Grocery Store to sell their eggs and cream. They buy groceries and gossip. They have kerchiefs tied over the metal curlers in their hair, so they'll look nice for Sunday morning mass. When Johnny Schaan closes his store for the night, they sit in their cars with the kids in front of Andy's waiting for the dads to come out.

My dad never goes to Andy's. He doesn't drink beer or vodka, which is Grandpa's favorite. I know because when Grandma isn't with us, Grandpa keeps a bottle in the cubby hole of the car and takes a sip every once in a while when we go for a ride in the country.

Sometimes Grandpa stops in at Andy's on the Soo Line payday. When he finally comes home for supper, holding onto the porch rail, putting one foot in front of the other carefully up the steps, Grandma leads him to the bedroom, talking mean in German all the way.

My dad doesn't go to Andy's on Saturday nights, and he doesn't go to Confession either because he's been Saved. He's accepted Jesus Christ as his personal savior. He doesn't need the priest. He can pray direct. He doesn't even have to sort his sins into venial and mortal, the kind that sends you straight to hell. Do not pass go. Do not stop at purgatory.

Grandma says to pray for Daddy every day, because he doesn't go to Mass, so I do—three Hail Marys. But the truth is—I like Daddy's gentle Jesus better than the Catechism God. Even if Daddy doesn't go to Mass to sit on the right side of Mount Carmel with the other men, we listen to Charles E. Fuller's "Old Fashioned Revival Hour" on Sunday nights:

"Heavenly sunshine, heavenly sunshine, flooding my soul with glory divine. Heavenly sunshine, heavenly sunshine, halleluiah, Jesus is mine."

After the program, Daddy reads me exciting stories from a big book with colored pictures of Samson and Delilah and David and Goliath.

It's really quiet in our apartment behind the Farmers Union Oil Company on the Saturday nights Mama works at the dance. Mama is a talker. She says so. She says she has to process things, and my dad is a good listener. But they don't talk on dance nights.

I hang around the bedroom when she's getting ready, wishing she didn't have to go. I bounce on the edge of the bed, until she tells me to stop it. She sits on a stool at her dressing table with the big mirror attached, and I lean my elbows on the edge, with my chin in my hands. I watch her put Ponds cold cream on her face with a sponge, then Max Factor liquid stuff, and finally a quick brush of powder from the blue-flowered china bowl. She lines her lips with a pencil and carefully fills in the lines with red lipstick. She draws black eyebrows on with a pencil too.

Then she sits on the bed. I stretch out on the feather pillows to watch her put her fist in her nylons, one at a time, checking for runs. She pulls each nylon from her toes up her leg, carefully so as not to get snags, and fastens them to the garters on her girdle. She stands up and turns her head around to make sure the seams are straight. When she clips earrings on, I know it's time for her to go.

The Farmers Union is open late on Saturday dance nights, so people can get gas and farm supplies, and Daddy has to work. He's just out front, but I hate being alone in the apartment.

Daddy's family doesn't believe in dancing, but we only see them a couple times a year. My best friend Antoinette's family is like that too. Her cousins in Harvey are Protestants. The Sisters say it is a sin to go into a Protestant church, but Antoinette and I have worked that all out. We go to our cousins' church when we visit them, but we don't confess it to Father Boniface. We make up for it by extra prayers at home. We set up boxes for altars in our bedrooms with little statues of the Blessed Mother. That's who women pray to mostly. The Blessed Mother understands women and will ask her Son to help you.

We pick crocuses in the field behind Antoinette's house to put in jelly glasses on our altars, and then we pray. We drape old curtains around our heads, make the sign of the cross, bow our heads, and kneel in front of our altar. We try to remember what Sister Mary Ellen says about striving for a prayerful attitude. If someone up there, God or the Blessed Mother or one of the Saints, is really watching, I want to be more devout than Antoinette.

After we practice being nuns, we rummage around on Mama's dressing table examining the makeup. "My mom says I can start wearing lipstick in 7th grade," Antoinette tells me for the hundredth time.

Then we put on the pink and yellow taffeta bridesmaid dresses my Aunt Fran gave me and wrap organdy curtains around our shoulders for stoles. We sweep into the living room singing, fluttering the long white curtains. We've seen *On Moonlight Bay* and *Tea for Two* at the Sunday matinee in Rugby and know the songs by heart. Doris Day is our idol—along with those girls the Blessed Mother appeared to at Fatima.

We dance around the living room. We float like clouds from the arms of the sofa, singing until we're breathless. Then we lean against the wall on my bottom bunk trying to decide what we should be. Nuns? Or Dancers?

Memoir published by *Dust & Fire,* spring, 2008

Thirteenth Summer

1953

Everything changed that summer. No more wiling away the long, hot days playing hopscotch and riding bikes with my best friend Antoinette. We were old enough to work. She had to take care of her little sisters and brother every day. I had a baby-sitting job on a farm.

I could still daydream my way through the boring care of a baby and a two-year-old, but helping Teresa Schaan wash milk separators and mounds of dirty dishes and pots and pans in the hot fly-filled kitchen was hard work and sullied my storybook illusions about marriage and any romantic ideas I had about living in the country. Just the winter before I'd taken care of the baby in Teresa and Johnny's apartment in town and mooned over them all dressed up for the Saturday night dance. They came home fondling each other, anxious for me to leave. I couldn't take my eyes off them. Now there was another baby, and they'd taken their place and family responsibilities in a small house on "the folks'" farm.

Previous summers Antoinette and I spent lazy afternoons exploring the gravel country roads beyond Balta on our bikes, baskets packed with chokecherry jelly sandwiches wrapped in waxed paper and grape nectar in quart jars. Warm with content, we ate our lunch on the concrete pedestal of the giant-sized crucifix in the cemetery. Now my precious blue and white deluxe Schwinn bike with the horn, 10th birthday gift from Grandpa, was abandoned in the tool shed.

I abandoned Grandma and Grandpa that summer too. Ordinarily, I walked to their house, four blocks from the apartment behind the Farmers Union store where I lived, every day, every season. If Grandma was rolling dough for *kuchen* or *kasnupla,* I stayed for supper. Grandpa entertained me with tall tales, illustrating with cartoon drawings on a yellow lined tablet. I sat with my chin in my hands, giggling, watching him sharpen his pencil with the knife he took out of the pocket in the bib of his overalls.

After supper the three of us sat at the kitchen table and played Chinese checkers. Grandpa always cheated. Grandma always chided with a smile, "Oh, Anton."

If Grandpa was reading when I got there, Grandma set me up with a crochet needle and thread to work on potholders. Grandpa was the only man I knew who read books other than the Bible, Dad's choice. "Westerns," Grandpa called his paperbacks. He didn't care for Mom's Book of the Month Club novels, but they shared copies of Louis L'Amour.

Some winter days after school, I walked down the street with my math book. Grandpa tutored me though he'd only gone through 8th grade himself. He considered himself fortunate to get that far. "Kids were needed on the farm when I was a boy," he enjoyed reminding me. "You're lucky. We could only go to school for a few months between fall harvest and spring planting." My grades were important to him. He was glad to help with math, and he paid me a nickel for every A on my report card.

Antoinette and I had spent many earlier grade school summer days in the play house Grandpa built me. The child-sized cupboards had doors and drawers, the drop leaf table a replica of the one he'd built for their house. He added doll beds and cradles on birthdays and Christmas.

Grandpa was tall and brawny—valuable physical attributes for work on the section crew of the Soo Line Railroad—and I was proud that he was the foreman. Other summers I often ran to meet him at the end of the work day at the section house near the railroad tracks. The crew quit work promptly at 5 p.m. After a sweating, strenuous day repairing railroad beds and replacing tracks, they called congenial "*gut nachts*," as they left the section house to walk home. Grandpa would pick up his black lunch pail with one hand and wrap my small hand in his other. I skipped beside him to keep up.

When Antoinette and I reminisce now about that time, she tells me that she was in agony with envy—of my play house, the Schwinn, and, most of all, my grandpa. Hers was old, crotchety, and barked at her when she made obligatory visits.

"Did you know Grandpa was the town drunk?" I ask her. She didn't know or doesn't remember. She dismisses my questions with, "All those German-Russian men drank a lot."

My mom worked at Andy's Tavern on Saturday dance nights, and I overheard her tell Dad that when she saw the tab Andy kept for Grandpa, she was "mortified." But she never talked to me about it, and I never told her that he had a bottle of schnapps in the cubby hole of his old Hudson. "Just a nip," he'd say and wink. "No need to tell *Grossmutter*."

Sometimes on payday Grandpa cashed his check at Andy's Tavern and treated all the men sitting at the bar. If he didn't come home for supper, Grandma sent me to Andy's. It was a dark, mysterious, man's place. On a hot summer day, the cool air and smell of beer met me like a big breath when I opened the door. I'd peer into the dark to see if Grandpa was sitting at the bar. Andy would see me. "Hey Tony, your kid's here."

We'd walk home together, my hand in his. Grandma would meet us at the door. He'd look over his shoulder at me with a silly grin and let her push him down the hallway to the bedroom, scolding him all the way. Her head barely reached his shoulders, but he never lifted his big hand against her.

As the years went by I didn't feel like skipping beside him if I happened to run into him on his way home from downtown in the early evening or a Saturday afternoon. He reeked of beer. I knew the scenario. Grandma would be meeting us at the door, muttering and scolding in German. The words were foreign, but the tone and meaning were clear.

German in our family was the language of secrets. Determined to be identified as "American," they didn't encourage me to learn German, and I certainly didn't want to be identified with the kids who spoke broken English. If Grandma and Mom were gossiping or discussing something they didn't want me to know about, they switched from English to German. They would discuss Grandpa's "problem" in German, then explain in English that he had the flu. I didn't believe that flu business much beyond 2nd grade, and I'd flounce off, angry with them for picking on him.

The summer I turned thirteen, Mom's sister Frances brought her husband to North Dakota to meet the family. Aunt Fran lived in Seattle and visited infrequently. Mom made remarks about her "honoring us with her presence." I wanted to grow up to be just like her—leave Balta, work at the Bon Marche' in Seattle, have long painted nails, and wear high-heeled shoes and suits to work every day.

I got up early that morning and spent the entire day at Grandma and Grandpa's house waiting for Aunt Fran and her husband to arrive. They finally drove up in a dark green car with big fins, chrome on the sides and chrome bullets on front and back bumpers. A silver-winged woman hood ornament. "Cadillac Seville," Dad muttered.

Aunt Fran opened her door and stepped out. She hugged me. "You are all grown up." Then she turned to the driver emerging from the chrome-draped car. "This is your Uncle Robbie."

I saw Gordon MacCrae. His long-sleeved shirt was open at the neck, the cuffs rolled up. He wore tan dress trousers and white shoes. I'd never seen a man like him except in the movies. And he informed us, without a hint of humor, that he'd "never seen anything like this flat, treeless prairie."

"Robbie asked, 'Is this it?' at every town from the Montana border," Aunt Fran gushed. "And when we turned off the paved highway, he said, 'Is this really a town?' "

I was grateful they were staying at Grandma and Grandpa's house. He might never have to know we didn't even have indoor plumbing in our apartment behind the Farmers Union.

Mom, Dad, Aunt Fran, and Uncle Robbie sat around the kitchen table getting acquainted. I sat on the floor, leaning against the counter absorbing it all, fascinated with this new uncle, and, as always, entranced by Aunt Fran. Grandma was bustling around at the kitchen counter washing green beans, slicing cucumbers, making supper. I glanced at the red plastic teapot clock on the wall above the table. It was way past five. Grandpa was late.

I heard his first step on the porch, then an eternity between each of the next four steps. *Hail Mary full of grace . . .* I could see him holding onto the railing. He opened the door and staggered in grinning. I didn't look at Mom or Grandma. I waited for the scold in a German-English duet. No one uttered a word.

I could get up and run out of the room crying. I'd played that distracting role before. A protest of loyalty. It didn't faze Mom, but Grandma always sympathized. "Ya, Niomi . . . so sensitive. You always stand up for him." I sat there with my back pressed against the cupboard, tears rolling down my cheeks. For the first time, I knew Mom's and Grandma's humiliation.

Memoir published by *The Talking Stick,* 2013

6

VADE IN PACEM

June, 2012

Antoinette encouraged me to join her at the Balta Centennial Celebration and All School Reunion. We had been enjoying email communications and summer reunions since the excursion I made to Balta with Vernice and Nick in 2007 when I found Antoinette's name in the guest book at Our Lady of Mount Carmel Church.

My bond with Antoinette is mysterious. I was immersed in an aura of contentment when we were together as children. That dormant affection struck me the minute she stepped out the door of their mobile home in our driveway five years ago.

I hadn't seen her for over fifty years.

We have followed different life paths. We don't share political views. We have had some testy dances with social issues. She lives in the south in a large white colonial house with a backyard swimming pool. I live in a pine-paneled cabin-remodeled-house in the woods of northern Minnesota. But, like me, she has been married to the same man for over fifty years. Her life centers on children and grandchildren. She's lost a son. I've lost a grandson. We wear aprons when we cook. She stands over me in my kitchen giving advice. She says, "I'm sorry. I'm so bossy."

I say, "I don't, mind." And I mean it.

I had disdained and disclaimed both Balta and my Catholicism for decades, blaming the nuns for all my insecurities and sharing the jokes with other ex-Catholics about our indoctrination in guilt. "*Mea culpa. Mea culpa.* We were raised Catholic."

My smug anti-Catholic stance had suffered a puncture wound a few years prior to the summer of 2012. After fifty years and oceans away from Our Lady of Mount Carmel and Balta, I had trembled and teared in Notre Dame Cathedral in Paris. There I realized the lifelong impact of the Mass, and, most of all, the bond, beyond death, with my mother and grandmother. Their presence overwhelmed me in that Cathedral.

Since that experience, I had dipped in and out of the holy water of the Catholic Church, always backing away because of the onerous social issues. But the influence of Balta and my German-Russian heritage hovered like a hag. I registered for the Centennial Celebration.

I arrive for the Saturday morning parade and park in a field of cars on the outskirts of the town. I walk a few blocks to Our Lady of Mount Carmel Church. Nothing is recognizable. Empty lots. Small, paint-peeling houses, little more than shacks.

I stop near a group of laughing, happy people, chatting, enjoying the camaraderie and the sunny June day. They glance at me, curious about the strange woman standing alone at the edge of the crowd on the sidewalk next to the church.

I have watched the Rose Bowl Parade in California, the Holidazzke parade in Minneapolis, Minnesota, numerous Memorial Day parades honoring our veterans, high school Homecoming parades, my kids marching in bands. But I have never witnessed this honoring of the land and of the farmers who first tilled it. I have never been proud of my heritage before.

I watch the gigantic tractors, combines, and other unrecognizable monstrous farm machinery chug by with banners waving—Mack Farms, Axtmann Farms, Schaan Farms, Klein Farms, Schmaltz Farms, all familiar names. Then trucks, parade floats of a sort, families seated on folding chairs in truck beds, waving to the crowd. Grandkids and great-grandkids of those homesteaders, jumping up and down, throwing Tootsie Rolls and bubble gum to their friends in the crowd lining the street. They hold banners: "John Axtmann Family," "In Memory of John and Theresa Schaan." I baby-sat for John and Theresa when they lived in an apartment behind the Standard Oil Service Station and then on their farm my thirteenth summer. Memories come in a flood. Inside, I am a hymn of joy.

As the parade ends, my cell phone rings. Antoinette is at the other end of Main Street. I weave my way through the crowds to meet her. There are only a handful of houses left on the block next to the church where I've been standing, none of them as big as I remember, including Antoinette's house across the street from the church.

Farther down on Main Street, Antoinette's hardware store is gone. The Standard Oil Service Station next to it is gone. The next block is occupied with tent canopies and displays lined up in rows along the grass. The small U.S. Post Office is no longer operational, but the building is open for this occasion. The elevators, depot, and railroad tracks are gone. The Soo Line Railroad Company abandoned Balta in 1969. All gone.

Main Street is a scattering of decrepit buildings, worn out, abandoned, revived today by the hundreds of people who have returned for this Centennial Celebration. Cars have been blocked from the street, but you can't walk a straight line from one side of the street to the other. The street is peopled with more of a roar than a buzz, punctuated by laughter and joyous shouts of recognition and hearty greetings. Antoinette grabs my hand. Duane takes hers, follows, halting to meet and greet, shake hands and hug. We weave in and out of the clusters of family and friends like a conga line.

This celebration is another side of the story. This reverence for the German-Russian homesteaders is part of the story I never considered in my quest for the truth of women's lives.

I run into my email friend, Don Schaan, who has come from San Francisco to celebrate with his siblings and extended family. None of his brothers or sisters had any desire to stay on the farm, he told me in a recent email.

From: Don Schaan
My mom and dad moved off of the farm, to Las Vegas, in 1985. They sold the approximate 10 acres, the house, barns, granaries, and yard were on. We have retained the approximately 1000 acres of hay and cropland. At the time we were growing up, that amount of acreage represented a high average size farmer. Now farmers have to have two and three times and more of acreage under their control in order to survive . . . The cropland is currently being farmed by a Schaan cousin who lives in the Balta area. To that extent it still remains among the direct descendants of Wilhelm . . . My great grandparents, Wilhelm and Eleanor Schaan immigrated from the Baltic Sea area of Russia in 1900.

Antoinette introduces me to her sisters and her brother, who have come from Montana, Minnesota, and Oregon. They were babies when I last saw them. She stops to introduce classmates I haven't seen since the early 1950s. We push through the crowd in the street to Andy's Bar, where there is standing room only.

"This is the first time I've been inside this place," I laugh with Antoinette. "My view was from a gap in the front door and a glimpse in the shadowy dark of the stools at the bar to see if Grandpa was sitting there . . . Oh yes, and standing at the side door of the attached dance hall, yearning to be one of the wedding guests twirling around to the 'Tennessee Waltz' and the 'Beer Barrel Polka' from the accordion on the stage. Or better yet, the bride."

Today you can't get to the bar, nor find a place to sit. The meet and greet of the street, the inching through the crowd goes on. Duane manages to push through to the bar and get us a beer. I am as awestruck and wide-eyed as a child.

At the end of the day, Antoinette's cousin Richard Schmaltz and his wife, Arlene Klein Schmaltz, invite us to join them for dinner at their home in Rugby, where they have retired. Like Richard and Antoinette, Arlene's great-grandparents emigrated from Odessa, Russia and homesteaded near Balta in 1898.

Four of Richard and Arlene's five college-educated children work in the business world beyond Pierce County and North Dakota. Their oldest son, Blaine, owns the 4th generation Schmaltz farm. Richard's grandfather, Augustine Schmaltz, homesteaded the quarter of land in 1898. Blaine farms the original homestead, the other Schmaltz land inherited by Antoinette and her siblings, as well as his own considerable acreage. In addition to the small grain crops of his father and grandfathers, he grows organic flax and is experimenting with non-glutinous wheat. His children are in college.

A letter from Arlene Klein Schmaltz—My grandfather Clemens Klein came to the Balta community in 1898. They came from New York on train to South Dakota. There they travelled with other families by horse and wagon to somewhere around Napoleon, ND. They had relatives there who had already settled. They got food and help to come to the Balta area. My grandma and grandpa homestead the land west of Balta. They put up a sod house. Their relatives in Napoleon had given them two cows so they would have milk. My father was Frank Klein. He had seven brothers and two sisters. His mother died at age 42 from an abscessed tooth. Grandfather then married a woman with four small children. The house was too small, so my father and his brothers slept in the hay loft of the barn. My dad always said how terribly cold it was in the winter . . .

The Richard Schmaltz/Arlene Klein home is buzzing. Sons and sons-in-law are setting up tables in the spacious living room, the family room, and on the flower-bedecked patio. The dining room seats twelve easily. The Wells Fargo executive daughter is pouring wine. Daughter-in-law Susan is putting bowls of food and stacks of plates on the granite kitchen island. (Antoinette moves close and whispers that Susan is not only Blaine's partner on the farm, but she is on the Rugby

School Board.) Teenage grandkids, some home from college for the occasion, bring in pizza and fried chicken to add to the food Arlene prepared ahead of time. Petite and vivacious Arlene, her smiles reaching to her flashing dark eyes, is everywhere—directing, greeting, welcoming in this big kitchen open to the dining room on one side and the living room on the other. A place designed for frequent large family gatherings. Arlene plates the sweets she baked weeks ago. Takes German potato salad out of the refrigerator. Forty people fill their plates. The old German-Russians, like myself, empty the potato salad bowl. The *kuchen* disappears.

This is a long way from Great Grandpa's homestead *and* from Odessa, Russia.

The next morning, the small resident congregation and their families serve breakfast in the basement of Our Lady of Mount Carmel. My cousin, Keith Axtmann, son of Vernice and Nick, is taking tickets. He tells me that the priest who comes every other Sunday to say Mass has revived the church. The Bishop from Fargo has determined that Mount Carmel must be preserved, and a handful of farmers, like Keith, who lives on the Axtmann homestead, have donated thousands of dollars. He points proudly to recent structural renovations.

I sit at a white-clothed table with fresh flower centerpieces. My grandmother's spirit sits with me. She cooked and served weddings feasts in this basement. I could wander in and out of the church kitchen on those days, smug, privileged—the cook in charge was my *grossmutter.*

"You had to take charge of the cooking . . . two women to do it . . . we mostly got $10 and then they went around with the plate—donate for the cook," she had told me.

The German-Russian weddings were all-day affairs. High Mass in the morning. Then dinner at the church—chicken, mashed potatoes and gravy, corn, pickles, and always *kuchen*. Wedding *kuchen* had a thin, flaky, pie-like crust with just a touch of cream and sprinkle of cinnamon and sugar, unlike the bread dough crust and thick custard of everyday *kuchen*.

Grandma baked it the day before the wedding. Sweet smell of cinnamon would greet you at her kitchen door. The counter would be covered with pans. When the *kuchen* had baked, she covered it with clean, bleached-white, dish towels. If I happened to wander in, I might get to sample one piece of the flaky bit of heaven.

After the Nuptial Mass and noon dinner, the dance began at the dance hall next door to Andy's bar and across the street from where I lived. The accordion music drifted out all day, and you could stand in the doorway and get a glimpse of the bride in her gown dancing by. Polkas, waltzes, schottisches. I yearned to be invited to one of those weddings. I wished my parents had more friends.

After an afternoon of dancing, the guests proceeded back to the church where my sergeant-in-the-kitchen grandma and another woman had prepared supper—homemade buns, sausage, bologna, cheese, German potato salad.

Then the wedding party and guests danced past midnight, though I didn't witness that. I only heard from my cynical dad about the drunken guests, the tipsy groom, and the bedraggled bride, sans veil, the bottom of her white dress dirty and torn, dancing until the last hat was passed.

By 8:30 every pew in Our Lady of Mount Carmel Church is filled for the Mass—three hundred men, women, and children, separated neither by sex nor age, sitting together on each side of the center aisle. From the choir loft, Vincent Schaan's adult grandchildren are singing.

And He will raise you up on eagle's wings/Bear you on the breath of dawn/ Make you to shine like the sun/And hold you in the palm of His Hand.

I had never heard those familiar words and music in this church. Such music was forbidden in my Catholic years. I last heard *And He will raise you up . . .* at my thirteen-year-old grandson's funeral. It is a portentous Prelude to the last scene of this reunion drama.

Monsignor Joseph Senger emerges from the sacristy, the mysterious room next to the altar that girls never entered in my day. He genuflects before the crucifix above the front altar in the apse, his right arm supported on the knee touching the floor. He makes the Sign of the Cross with deliberation, forehead, heart, left shoulder, right. *In the name of the Father, the Son, and the Holy Ghost.* He stands, turns, and steps slowly and carefully down from the altar to the Communion rail. Then he looks up and strides down the center aisle of the church with a broad smile. He greets people on each side, shaking hands with the men, clasping the hands of women and children in his.

Impulsively, I step into the aisle from my pew. The energy of his crushing hug takes me by surprise, and I return it with unexpected emotion.

"Niomi," he says, with a wide, surprised smile. "What are *you* doing here? Oh yes . . . yes . . . you grew up here," he recalls.

In his eighties now, Father Joe resembles my grandmother with the sharp prominent nose, narrow lips, and distinctive small, slightly slanted dark eyes of the Sengers. I hear Grandma's English with the German accent in the rhythm of his words. They are one. She is here. Love and loss, joy and sorrow all pour from me like those plaster statues in our church myths who wept.

Father Joe returns to the altar. The Mass is not as I remember it. He faces the congregation from a table altar set just behind the Communion rail, thus closer to the congregation than the priest in my past who stood with his back to us at the imposing altar in the apse. Unlike the Latin muttering I remember, Father Joe chants and prays with a strong, emphatic, earnest voice.

In the name of the Father, and of the Son, and of the Holy Spirit . . . Lord, have mercy. Christ, have mercy. Lord, have mercy.

I am missing the comfort and familiarity of Latin.

Kyrie eliason/Christi eliason/Kyrie eliason.

Our Lady of Mount Carmel is filled with Schmaltzes and Schalls and Axtmanns, Kleins, and Schaans, 3rd and 4th generations of the families who homesteaded here. Germans from Russia have returned *heim* for this celebration. They have come from everywhere in the United States.

Gunda Massine, a former classmate, and significant for me, a woman, reads the Epistle. Father Joe steps to the lectern and welcomes the congregation—in English.

In my childhood, Father Boniface's sermons, first in German, then in English, gave the child me an interminable hour to wander into the lives of the Saints. I could gaze at the stained glass windows from my pew—Mary's mother, the beautiful St. Anne, and the veiled St. Rose, with her crown of thorns. St. Rose took a vow of virginity and devoted her life to prayer and penance.

Father Joe recognizes his connection to Balta, noting that he took the train from Orrin, North Dakota (ten miles away), to live with his Aunt Lena and Uncle Anton (my grandparents) and attend high school in Balta. He was able to become a priest, he says, because of that opportunity. He gives some history of the church and its founders.

He returns to the altar. Facing the congregation, he blesses the bread and wine. He raises the host and the chalice toward the heavens:

Holy, Holy, Holy . . . Sanctus, Sanctus, Sanctus . . .

I wait for the invitation to Communion and the caveat, "Only baptized Catholics."

"Come to the Communion rail as you do every Sunday," he says—without a proviso.

Antoinette motions for me to stand up and move out of the pew.

"Are you going?"

"Yes, and you are too," she whispers.

The pews empty—in order and without ushers. Two lines of men, women, and children move down the center aisle to the Communion rail. How many practicing Catholics in these hundreds who have come Home from everywhere is anyone's guess, but today we are all Catholic and joyously so.

Walking back to my pew on the side aisle, host dissolving on my tongue, my hands remember and fold. "Eyes down, an attitude of prayer," Sister Mary Ellen taught in first grade. It becomes prayer.

Father Joe's last words, "Go in Peace," *Vade in Pacem*—Finale.

The German-Russian Catholic settlers, after arriving in the New World, as a rule stayed for a few weeks with some friends and relatives who had established a new home already. Thus the majority of our Catholic people had friends in the town of Eureka, Aberdeen, Ipswich, all in South Dakota. From there they moved across the border into North Dakota . . . in what is today Emmons County and McIntosh County. However, droughts, poor land, and consequently poor crops induced our pioneers to look for a more promising location with better prospects of livelihood. Several of the men were, therefore, delegated as scouts for explorers to the territory of the present Pierce County . . .

The new settlement began at once in 1899. The influx of Catholic settlers kept on steadily until the year 1902.

All pioneers underwent unspeakable hardships and privations. This so much so that some of them entertained the plan to return again either to Germany, from where their grandparents had come or to South Russia. Conditions were more than primitive; conveniences there were none whatsoever. Travelling was carried on with some rickety wagon and very often with a stone boat which was drawn by a pair of oxen. Thus, moving from McIntosh County to the present Pierce County took them over two weeks. It was late in the year; blizzards overtook them on the open prairie, their only shelter being a wagon-box and a few blankets.

On their way here several children died and were buried on the lonely prairie. Weeping and almost heartbroken the pioneers stood around the graves, which they had a hard time to dig, and recited the Rosary, blessed the graves with their year and a Sign of the Cross and then they moved on. Later on they were able to rediscover some of those resting places and the remains were transferred into blessed ground . . .

Reaching their destination in present Pierce County at last, the open prairie was their abode, the sky their shelter and the wagon-box their only room, until a sod house had been built.

Historical Record of Our Lady of Mount Carmel Church, Balta, North Dakota
by the Reverend Monsignor Boniface Stuetz, 1938

EPILOGUE

Our Lady of Mount Carmel Church is the only thing left in this community that resembles anything in my memory. But what I realize today is that it represents more than the embodiment of Catholicism.

Most homes in Balta were spare, few adorned with more than crocheted doilies on the back and arms of a sofa and a crucifix, with braided palm leaves, on the wall. Hard work was Life for farm people and town people. Except for a few affluent farmers and merchants, there was just enough money for food, coal for the furnace, and a small closet.

We had no museums or concert halls. School *was* basic. School *was* reading, writing, and arithmetic. No band or orchestra, or art or music appreciation classes.

But here in Our Lady of Mount Carmel, we had sculpture modeled after Michelangelo and Giotto, paintings after Raphael and da Vinci. We had poetry in the prayers and Gregorian chants of the Mass. Sunday after Sunday after Sunday, music and poetry. Here in this church we had the colors of life—the violet of penance and melancholy, the red of passion and martyrdom, and, most of all, the white of glory and joy. We had pomp and circumstance in processions and celebrations. We had theatre in the stories of the faith.

A daydreaming child could be transported to another world through the rhythmic monotony and intonation of the High Mass even with the nauseous incense floating from the thurible. The stained glass windows could come to life, embodiments of metaphor and simile.

Here in the traditions and the Mass and the mantra of the Rosary, adults found an hour or two of peace and rest. Here the ritual and the routine of life in Balta, determined by Our Lady of Mount Carmel, grounded even the most anxious child. And the child absorbed things beyond dogma that fill the spirit forever.

We are all the people we ever were. I'm all the ages I ever was. And in old age, this childhood transcends adult skepticism.

ACKNOWLEDGMENTS

My appreciation to the editors of the following publications in which parts of this work were previously published: *Day In, Day Out—Women's Lives in North Dakota,* University of North Dakota press, *1988; Among Women; Lake Region Review; Dust and Fire; The Talking Stick; Winter on the Prairie.*

Thanks to editor, Angela Foster. Any boring exposition, excessive use of passive voice, or confusing tense are not her responsibility.

Special thanks to Antoinette Schmaltz Klevgard for lifelong friendship and precious memories; to Don Schaan for sharing his reflections and his research, his art and his photographs; to Arlene Klein Schmaltz for warm welcome and sharing her family story.

Thanks to my writing friends in Bards, Jackpine Writers' Bloc, and Twigs who read parts of this manuscript with criticism and encouragement. Special thanks to Kathy Medellin, whose North Dakota roots and extensive work in genealogy, gives her a unique insight; and to her sister, artist Bickey Bender, for capturing our place on canvas and giving me permission to use "Always the Tracks" on the cover.

Thanks to creative women extraordinaire: Sharon Harris for meticulous reading and copy editing and Tarah Wolff for format and design.

Made in the USA
Charleston, SC
10 June 2014